WORLD FAMOUS
DICTATORS

WORLD FAMOUS
DICTATORS

Ian Schott
with Damon Wilson

Constable & Robinson Ltd
3 The Lanchesters
162 Fulham Palace Road
London W6 9ER

This edition published by Magpie Books,
an imprint of Constable & Robinson Ltd 2004

First published in the UK by Magpie Books 1992

A copy of the British Library Cataloguing in Publication Data
is available from the British Library.

ISBN 978-1-84529-032-0

1 3 5 7 9 10 8 6 4 2
B paperback
Printed and bound in the EU

Contents

Introduction: Ancient Rome: the Cradle of Dictatorship   1

Chapter one: Papa Doc: Voodoo Gangster   27

Chapter two: The Emperor Caligula: Blood and Poison   44

Chapter three: Idi Amin: Monster from the Ashes   55

Chapter four: Genghis Khan: Sacker of Cities   70

Chapter five: Nicolae Ceaucescu: A Family Affair   81

Chapter six: Ivan The Terrible: Sacrifices to Cronus   94

Chapter seven: Emperor Bokassa I:
   The Napoleon of Bangui   110

Chapter eight: Adolf Hitler:
   The Revenge of a Failed Artist   121

Chapter nine: Vlad Dracul: The Impaler Strikes Back   144

Chapter ten: Stalin: The Bureaucractic Killer   154

Chapter eleven: Saddam Hussein:
   The Butcher of Baghdad   171

Ancient Rome: the Cradle of Dictatorship

The Beginnings of the Dictator

It might be thought that dictatorship is as old as humanity – a simple case of an Alpha male wielding a club to defeat the other males and win control of the caveman tribe. But a dictator is more than a tribal leader or even, in most cases, a king.

The title was invented by the ancient Romans, and designated an *appointed* leader in times of crisis. The dictator (a Latin term that amounted to emergency commander) was granted special powers by the free Roman people, because it was recognized that hard times often demanded quick decisions, unimpeded by senatorial debate. The position was not supposed to be hereditary. Rome, after all, was a republic, and hereditary power was the hallmark of a king (a concept pathologically hated by the Romans). After the crisis was over, it was stipulated, the dictator would revert back to a normal citizen's position, and absolute rule would return to the Senate.

The Roman Republic is long-gone, but the idea of the dictator has lingered on like the smell of old blood. Of course the original, idealistic course of events has not always gone astray – British prime ministers and US presidents, for example, have often been granted near dictatorial powers during major wars, but none have (so far) refused to give them up again. The dictators in this book, however, all seized power – one way or another – then held onto it by claiming a *permanent* state of emergency. The fact that such ongoing emergencies were, almost invariably, the result of their own brutality, corruption or war-mongering just goes to show the danger of absolute power: it is an addictive drug, for which the addict will commit any crime.

But how did the Romans – a people, by their own lights, more noble than any other – produce this strange hybrid: a freely elected absolute ruler? The answer lies in the early days of Roman history, before they even called themselves an empire.

The Republic

The Romans were probably an offshoot of the Latin tribes on the Mediterranean peninsula known to the Greeks as *Vitelliu*, or "calf-land", because they saw it as ideal dairy country. Later the first and last letters of the name were dropped, giving us *Itelli* or Italy. Rome, situated halfway down the peninsula on inland hills flanking the River Tiber, was probably founded around 900 BC.

For the first few centuries Rome was just another little hill town. The Latins were a hard-headed, practical and, most importantly, a disciplined people but, from the first, they were overawed by Greek culture and Greek subtlety, and set out to learn all they could from them. They adopted the Greek gods, only changing their names: *Zeus* to *Jupiter* and *Eros* to *Cupid*, for example. The Romans even paid the Greeks the compliment of co-opting a little of their history, claiming that Rome was founded by Aeneas, the Trojan prince who fled from the Greeks after the fall of Troy.

Another version of early Roman history, as recounted by the nineteenth century historian Winwood Reade, declared that "a rabble of outlaws and runaway slaves banded together, built a town, fortified it strongly, and offered it as an asylum to all fugitives. To Rome fled the over-beaten slave, the thief with his booty, the murderer with blood red hands. This city of refuge became a war town . . . its citizens alternately fought and farmed; it became the dread and torment of the neighbourhood." And, like the boomtowns in the American Wild West, Rome started with a lot more men than women, so the Romans kidnapped all the women of the nearby Sabine tribe. It is an interesting story; for this tale of the founding of Rome by brutalized slaves, ruthless murderers and pragmatic rapists helps to explain a certain fatal deficiency in the Roman soul – a curious insensitivity and literal-mindedness. The Romans never learned to inhabit the world of imagination as the Greeks did.

The Roman hatred of kings dated from a period in their early, almost mythological history, when they were conquered by a non-Latin people from the north of Italy. The Etruscans were originally an Asiatic people, possibly survivors of the Hittite Empire that collapsed around the same time as the fall of Troy (around 1200 BC). If so, of course, the Etruscans would have had a better claim to be the descendants of the Asiatic Prince Aeneas than the Romans had, and we may speculate that the Romans simply stole an Etruscan origin myth.

Little is known about the Etruscans – their language has yet to be deciphered – but, according to Roman histories, they were as artistic as the Greeks, but with a taste for decadent pleasures tempered by a gloomy pessimism that completely clashed with the attitude of their Roman subjects. The Etruscans set up a puppet monarchy to rule Rome, but the Etruscan kings made themselves so unpopular that, around 509 BC, the Romans not only drove them out, but also swore never to be ruled by a line of monarchs again.

The Roman decision to become a republic flew in the face of virtually every other Mediterranean culture, where monarchs were the norm. Only the Athenian Greeks – Rome's political and cultural icon – had experimented with, to modern eyes, very limited democracy. Yet it would be wrong to think of the Republican Romans as true democrats or egalitarians. They were a class-stratified society – aristocratic patricians looked down on the working-class plebeians, and even plebeians ruthlessly exploited the numerous slaves who soon became the backbone of Rome's growing economy. The Romans, who initially restricted the right to vote to patrician senators alone, believed that few limits should be placed on the mistreatment of those lower than oneself. Yet, importantly, they fiercely refused to allow any one individual to rise to be permanently higher than all his fellow citizens. They were egalitarian only in their shared hatred of would-be kings.

To maintain the balance of power (in non-emergency situations) two consuls (ruling magistrates) held separate but equal powers and could, if acting together, overrule the decisions of the senate. To stop any one individual getting too settled to such power, consuls were elected yearly, and no individual could rule for two years consecutively. Thus the post of dictator was actually the short-term combination of the dual office of the consuls. A logical enough step, provided dictatorial power could be removed from an individual after the time of crisis had passed.

As well as copying limited democratic government from the Athenian Greeks, the early Romans also developed a strong belief in honour and decency. Possibly their brush with the near-decadent Etruscans had sickened them but, for whatever reason, a noble Roman was expected to be frugal, hard-working, brave, honest, serious (being a good dancer, for example, was considered the height of debauchery) and, above all, loyal to Rome. This was an almost unheard of level of self-denial in the ancient Mediterranean. To find a similarly strict code of living, one has to look as far afield as Confucian China, Puritan New England or middle-class Victorian London. In fact, as we will see, the Romans rarely lived up to this idealistic self-image, but they found that actually maintaining such high standards was unnecessary. As their power and wealth grew, they continually told each other that they were clearly the best people in the world – what else could be the explanation for their unprecedented success? Yet, at the same time, many Romans indulged in the sort of treachery, corruption and debauchery that would have scandalized an Etruscan king. But the continually reinforced illusion of "honourable Rome" was enough – and it proved to be a driving force behind the Roman military expansion.

In 494 BC, the plebeians, angry at class injustice, all marched out of Rome up the River Tiber and declared that they would simply found another city unless they were given some rights. This mass withdrawal of organized labour had the desired effect, and the patricians were forced to grant the people their own representatives (called tribunes) in the government of the city. Theoretically the tribunes could overrule the Senate, but this rarely happened as the plebeians were usually manipulated into fighting among themselves rather than standing up for their rights or those who fought for them.

For example, in 486 BC a patrician named Spurius Cassius proposed to grant the plebeians the right to public land. The patricians rose as one man; Cassius was accused of wanting to become king and was executed. The tribunes (patricians themselves) did nothing to save him. And later, in 440, when a rich plebeian named Spurius Maelius tried to become a popular leader during a famine by lowering the price of his corn, he was summoned before a hastily appointed dictator and executed. To pacify the people, his corn was distributed free; those who talked of avenging his death were quietly disposed of.

Here we see the original use of the Roman dictator – the tool of the Senate, rather than vice versa: a hanging judge elected to do the dirty work of the ruling party. It was not until later that the Senate found itself forced to be the tool of the dictator.

Another temporary dictator, Marcus Manlius, became a national hero when he saved the Capitol (the senatorial seat of government) during a sneak attack on Rome by Gaulish (French) barbarians in 390 BC – every schoolboy used to know the story of how the geese sounded the alarm. Following the Gaulish retreat and his return to being an ordinary citizen, Manlius was saddened by the spectacle of ex-soldiers being thrown in jail for debt, and began freeing such debtors with his own private fortune. Aghast at this spectacle of embarrassing altruism, the patricians accused him of wanting to become a king and incited the plebeians to sentence him to death. Manlius was thrown from the Tarpeian Rock – a cliff on the very Capitoline Hill that he had so bravely defended.

The Seeds of Empire

Most of Roman aggressive energy, however, was directed outward, towards their unfortunate neighbours and further afield. It didn't take long to bring the rest of the Italian peninsula under Roman rule, including Etruria, the home of their old enemies, the Etruscans.

Rome's next challenge was Carthage. Originally a colony city of the Middle Eastern people called the Phoenicians, Carthage sat on the African coast, in what is now Tunisia, directly opposite the toe of Italy, and its sea trade easily outdistanced that of inland Rome. Perhaps the civilized thing to do would have been to build better ports on the Italian coast to compete with Carthage properly, but the Romans didn't think that way. In 264 BC, Rome broke a treaty with Carthage and invaded Sicily (a Greek colonized island that Carthage ruled as a protectorate). It is possible that the Romans had convinced themselves that Carthage would be a pushover – the Phoenicians were a trading race, disinclined to bloodshed – but the Punic Wars (*Punic* meaning Phoenician) raged, on and off, for the next 118 years, and, at one point, almost finished Rome completely.

In 218 BC, Hannibal of Carthage led an army (famously including African elephants) through Spain and southern France, then over the Alps into northern Italy and Roman home territory – the first such invasion since the Gaulish incursion. Hannibal was a master tactician and defeated the Romans again and again. At the Battle of Cannae alone, Rome lost 66,000 men to Hannibal's losses of just 6,000. In the end, nothing stood between Hannibal and besieging Rome herself: nothing, that is, but the meanness of the Carthaginians. Despite his amazing run of successes, the people of Carthage starved his army of men and supplies. He thus could not deliver the knockout blow, and the Romans eventually rallied and drove him out of Italy. Then they invaded North Africa and thrashed the Carthaginians completely. Even Hannibal advised a ceasefire.

If the Carthaginians had not realized their war with Rome was a life-and-death struggle, the Romans were under no such illusion. Following the ceasefire, Rome set out to finish the contest once and for all. One influential senator, Cato the Censor, ended every speech to the Senate, on whatever the subject, with the words: "And I will say furthermore, my fellow Senators, Carthage must be destroyed!"

Yet the shame that they had to bully and trick the now weakened and largely defenceless Carthage into a final war was not lost on the Romans. Neither was the inhumanity of not only enslaving the entire surviving population, but the total removal of Carthage from the map. Later Roman historians often referred to the "Punic curse" when they described some lapse of Roman honour: they apparently understood just how callous the endless wars had made them, but the dividends were too good to lose. The Punic Wars turned Rome into a ruthless fighting machine, and nobody could stand up for long against Roman interests and arms.

By 100 BC Rome had overrun the Mediterranean; they had added Greece, Spain and the Balkans to their list of conquests. They even took Macedonia, the country of Alexander the Great. Wealth was flooding in from all sides. Everyone benefited; the plebeians were always being given free handouts and treated to public shows in which captives had to fight for their lives against lions, leopards and each other. The urban workers were not going to complain about the increasing power of the rich so long as the rich kept them so well entertained. In a city as wealthy as Rome, there was plenty for everyone. This would have been fine if they were just a city-state, like Athens or Sparta, but Rome was now greater than a city – it was an empire in all but name.

Dictators

What worried men like Tiberius Gracchus and his brother Gaius, grandsons of the great Punic War general Scipio Africanus, was that most of the wealth and land was passing into the hands of a few people, and that these were mostly ruthless and corrupt. Rome's greatness had been founded on small farmers who owned their own land; such men might have a few slaves, but these were treated almost as members of the family. Now, just as in the time of Marcus Manlius, soldiers returning from border wars were being jailed for petty debts and the small farms were being gobbled up by wealthy landowners.

These new super farms were being stocked with armies of slaves by Mediterranean pirates who raided coastal settlements and captured hapless sea traders. And the cheap grain produced by mass slave labour was putting the remaining small farmers out of business. The fields were full of chained slaves who were bred and branded like cattle. Naturally, these escaped whenever they could, and went around committing robbery and murder until they were caught and tortured to death. For example, in 134 BC, seventy thousand slaves revolted and took over the island of Sicily. The Romans killed them all, but not before the island was ravaged. A happy and contented country was turning into a land of suffering and brutality.

In the year of the slave revolt in Sicily, Tiberius Gracchus was elected tribune of the people. His first act was to propose a law to limit the amount of land that could be held by a single family. He suggested too that land should be given to homeless ex-soldiers (many of whom had spent twenty or thirty years serving Rome for very little pay). This was too much for the patricians. His fellow senators rose up against him, chased him into the street, and beat him to death with table legs. Ten years later, his brother Gaius – another "troublemaker" – was forced to commit suicide for suggesting similar reforms. The ideal of democratic republicanism was rapidly decaying into plutocratic autocracy – the rich ruled like despots, under a thin disguise of public responsibility.

Under such self-serving guidance, Rome was slipping into violence by a process of endless self-justification. The phrase *Pax*

Romana (Roman peace) had originally been used to indicate Rome's intention of civilizing neighbouring states for the good of all – Roman magistrates, for example, had once travelled to distant countries like the Balkans to hand out unbiased justice as their gift and example to uncivilized barbarians. But after the Punic Wars, *Pax Romana* increasingly came to indicate "surrender to the will of Rome or be crushed".

It would be wrong to imply that Rome's allies, and even those that Rome had conquered, did not ultimately prosper under Roman domination: the Roman sword spread classical Greek ideals of civilization to Western Europe, Asia Minor, the Middle East and North Africa. The *Pax Romana* encouraged trade, spread superior agricultural techniques and educated warrior tribes to live, as most Roman citizens did most of the time, in peace. The time of the Roman Republic and, later, the Roman Empire, can generally be seen as a golden age in human history. But those that dared to resist Rome or, worse, insulted Roman honour, were shown little mercy. The Roman historian Tacitus later quoted the bitter speech of a Celtic war chief, Calgacus, facing a Roman land and sea invasion and certain annihilation:

> Pillagers of the whole world, they have exhausted the land through their indiscriminate plundering, so now they ransack the sea. A rich neighbour only excites their greed; a weak neighbour their lust to dominate. All the East and West did not glut their hunger. They are unique in their violent craving to despoil the poor as well as the wealthy. They steal, butcher, rape and they call it empire; they make a desolation and call it peace.

And once a nation – or an individual – has started down this particular slope of idealized, self-justified brutality, it is almost impossible to apply the brakes. The Roman people were too unimaginative and short-sighted to realize that, once murder has been justified on grounds of expediency, it can become a habit, then a disease. Up to around 100 BC, the victims of Rome's violent contagion had mostly been conquered foreigners (and a few Roman would-be reformers) but the wind of history then began to blow it back onto its creators.

Marius and Sulla

Ironically, the man who was most responsible for bringing the infection of tyrannous dictatorship home to Rome was not a criminal or degenerate; in fact, he originally possessed all the Roman virtues. Gaius Marius was the son of a farm labourer; he rose to eminence in the army, married a patrician girl, and succeeded in getting himself elected tribune (a spokesman for plebeian rights). He was in his mid-forties when an African general named Jugurtha rose up in revolt. Jugurtha's skill in guerrilla warfare enabled him to defy the might of Rome for four years. Finally, Marius marched off to try his luck. He soon decided to abandon force in favour of treachery. Jugurtha's father-in-law was bribed to betray him, and lure him into a trap laid by a brilliant young officer known as "Lucky Sulla". Marius was able to keep his promise to drag Jugurtha back to Rome in chains. The angry populace tore off the captive's jewels and clothes, yanking the ear-rings so violently that they ripped the flesh. Jugurtha was thrown into an icy dungeon and executed a few days later. Marius became the most popular man in Rome, and was awarded a triumph (a military parade in his honour through the streets of Rome). This was the highest honour a Roman citizen could officially be given.

Rome undoubtedly needed Marius. Barbarian invaders, like the Gauls and the German Goths (making their first appearance in history) were attacking the frontiers from the north. A Roman army had been virtually wiped out at Arausio, on the Rhône – the most shattering defeat since Hannibal. Marius was hastily despatched to meet the Goths as they poured into Italy. Fortunately, the barbarians had divided their forces. Marius drove the Teuton tribe back into Aix en Provence, where he annihilated them; then he caught up with the other half, the Cimbri tribe, and routed them at Vercellae, near Milan.

Once again, Marius was the hero of Rome. He was elected consul for the sixth consecutive year – a glorious but illegal achievement, since each of the two consuls was only supposed to serve for a year at a time.

To consolidate his position, Marius joined forces with two popular, reformist demagogues, Saturninus and Glaucia, and set out to topple the conservative element of the Senate and enforce plebeian rights. The fact that this reformist revolution would also make him unassailably powerful must also have occurred to him. Unfortunately, Marius' talents as a politician were mediocre – a military man with no patrician "breeding", his manners were too blunt and harsh. He also foolishly tried to intrigue with both sides at once and lost most of his friends and allies in the process. The planned reformation was a total failure; as soon as he began to throw his weight around, anti-Marius riots were orchestrated by the reformers and, as consul, he was forced to call out the army. The mob, quickly swapping to Marius' side now they saw the drawn swords, then chased their former leaders into the Capitol building and tore them apart.

It was a hollow victory for Marius. His shot at making himself a permanent dictator had merely destroyed his own power base. Suddenly, the "saviour of Rome" found himself a political has-been. It had all happened so quickly – within a month or two of his victorious return – that he found it difficult to grasp. He had always had an imperious temper; now he became suspicious and paranoid.

But the conservatives had also overreached themselves. There really was an urgent need for reform – not just in Rome but in the whole of Italy. The people needed champions to defend them against the wealthy; but as soon as a champion appeared, he was murdered.

When this happened to another reformer named Drusus, Italy flared into civil war. Once again, Marius was needed. He and his old subordinate "Lucky Sulla" – now his bitter rival – were placed in command of the armies and marched off to slaughter men who had once fought under them – mostly dissatisfied Italians who felt they had a right to become full Roman citizens.

At this point, a king named Mithridates of Pontus – on the southern coast of the Black Sea – decided to seize this opportunity to acquire himself an empire. He invaded Syria and Asia Minor and sent out secret orders that all Romans living in conquered cities should be put to death. When the day came, more than a hundred thousand men, women and children were dragged out into the streets and massacred.

The people of Rome were shattered by the news – it seemed incredible that Romans could be treated as they had treated their conquered enemies, as mere cattle. The rich were even more shaken by loss of revenues from eastern trade and taxes. Thanks to the civil war at home the treasury was empty. The Senate decided that, instead of slaughtering the Italians, it might be a better idea to give them what they wanted and then send them to fight Mithridates. So the Italians finally achieved their full Roman citizenship.

It might be assumed that, in the face of the Asian threat, Rome would cease its internal squabbles. But the Romans had become too accustomed to quarrelling amongst themselves. To begin with, Marius and Sulla both thought they ought to have the honour of destroying Mithridates. The Senate preferred the patrician Sulla. So Marius threw in his lot with a popular demagogue named Sulpicius, who appealed directly to the plebeians. They not only voted him command of the army; they also went off looking for Sulla to tear him to pieces. Sulla had to flee from Rome. But he fled to his soldiers – the ones who had helped him to put down the Italian rebellion – and marched on Rome. After some bitter fighting, it was Marius' turn to flee. His friend Sulpicius was caught and executed while Marius headed to exile in Africa. Having settled this little quarrel, Sulla had himself voted dictator, murdered a few hundred of Marius' supporters, passed some laws, and finally marched off to fight Mithridates.

Ancient Rome: the Cradle of Dictatorship

The moment Sulla's back was turned, however, Marius hurried back to Rome. Vengeful, eaten up with jealousy and hatred, he behaved like a maniac. Like Sulla, he had his faithful army – his soldiers liked to call themselves "Marius' mules" – and he now began a reign of terror such as Rome had never seen before. He had the gates of the city closed, then ordered his men to kill all his "enemies" – that is, anyone against whom he nursed a grudge. And since a paranoid man has a grudge against half the world, thousands of Rome's most distinguished men died in those few days. When Marius walked through the streets, men hastened to salute him. If Marius looked the other way, it was a sign that the man was one of his enemies, and his soldiers cut him down on the spot.

Marius soon declined from vicious paranoia to total insanity. He began to find it impossible to sleep, even though he drank himself into a stupor every night. And after having himself elected consul for the seventh time running he fell into a fever and died. All Italy heaved a sigh of relief.

But the tyrant's death brought no deliverance. When Sulla arrived back in Rome – after forcing Mithridates to make peace – it suddenly became just as dangerous to have been one of those to whom Marius had acknowledged salutes. Another reign of terror began. Senators and officials were killed by the thousand and, very shortly, the murders ceased to be purely political. For, as all absolute rulers have discovered, it is hard to see the difference between a man you dislike for political reasons and a man you just happen to find dislikeable. After a while, it is not even necessary to dislike a man in order to kill him. If he has a desirable estate, and you want it for one of your friends, it seems natural to regard its owner as a tiresome obstacle. Beginning as the "liberator" of Rome, Sulla ended as its first dictator in the modern sense: a monster as head of state.

But, at the end, he lived up to his nickname of Lucky Sulla. Instead of suffering the typical fate of men who are universally hated and feared, he gave up the dictatorship, retired to his estate and died peacefully in his bed. As an old soldier, he presumably found politics boring and thus managed to break the addiction of total power. We may also suspect that he felt that the increasingly degenerate Romans were not worth the waste of his time. Sulla had been born in the days of the third Punic War, when Rome still believed itself proud, independent and democratic. Now most of the old breed were dead – many of them executed by Marius or himself – and the rest were like terrified sheep. The true decline of Rome had begun.

The Three-Headed Monster

The rest of the story of republican Rome is mainly one of criminal violence. After the death of Sulla, in 78 BC, the roads of civil-war-ravaged Italy, and even of Rome itself, were overrun with robbers. Wanton murder became commonplace and the sea was suddenly full of pirates – the historian Mommsen called it "the golden age of buccaneers". Romans, being hill men at heart, never made good sailors, so ran an inefficient navy. And with most of the Mediterranean's true sea powers, like Carthage and Greece, crushed or undermined by Roman bullying, the pirates had almost a free hand. Escaped slaves, bankrupt farmers and ex-soldiers and fleeing outlaws naturally took to the one way of life that allowed them to strike back at Rome, and many seaside communities helped them, gaining from their plunder and avoiding being sacked themselves.

Piracy became so bad that only about a third of the corn Rome imported from Africa and Egypt actually reached Roman ports. Pirate vessels were usually light craft with shallow draught and a formidable turn of speed. They could follow a merchantman at a distance, too low in the water to be seen, and attack by night – sometimes even following the merchantman into port, killing the man on watch and slipping out again before dawn loaded with plunder. Men and women were prized as much as other booty, for they could be sold as slaves. The Greek island of Delos became virtually one huge slave market, with tens of thousands of people changing hands every day.

The pirates were soon strong enough to demand "protection" money from major ports, and openly used them when they needed repairs. The province of Cilicia, in what is now southern Turkey, became the main pirate stronghold, but little buccaneer forts sprang up along the coasts on every sea lane.

Naturally, of course, the Roman plutocrats found a way to profit from all this misery and death. For a start, with grain supplies being so short, they were able to buy it all up, then sell it to the plebeians at grossly inflated prices. And with so many people being enslaved, the price of a slave dropped through the floor. It now became cheaper to work a slave to death on starvation rations, then buy another, than it was to maintain even minimal human living standards on the big slave farms. This latter policy, however, was to rebound on the slave masters.

Five years after the death of Sulla, a gladiator named Spartacus – a Greek deserter from the Roman army who had been caught and enslaved – escaped from the gladiator school at Capua and hid on Mount Vesuvius, together with a small band of other escapees. As other slaves heard about the group, they broke free and came to join them. Spartacus' band was soon big enough to attack and destroy the big local slave farms, freeing many more slaves to join them and costing the farm owners millions of gold pieces. The slave army knew they would all be tortured to death if they were recaptured, so they fought like demons against the Roman forces sent out against them and achieved a remarkable series of victories.

The Romans were stunned – they had come to believe that their armies were invincible and that slaves were little better than cowardly animals; now Spartacus was rumoured to be thinking of marching on Rome itself. Worse still, Rome had no competent general to send against the rebels – their best man, Pompey, was away in Spain fighting another rebellion. Eventually, the Romans decided to appoint a multimillionaire called Crassus – an opportunist who had made his fortune buying up the land of executed senators (the victims of Marius and Sulla and of numerous minor senatorial plots) and by setting up Rome's first (pay-to-use) fire brigade. Few doubted his canniness, but he had no military experience at all.

But Crassus was lucky. Their string of victories had turned the slave army into a murderous rabble whose only interests were pillage and rape. On a small scale, Spartacus' slaves were repeating the history of Rome: effort and determination leading to success, and success leading to degeneration and viciousness. Drunk with revenge and plunder, the slaves refused Spartacus' pleas to escape Italy by sea. He saw that the peninsula was a closed trap, with the city of Rome, to the north, blocking the only way out. Reluctantly, he marshalled his army to march north.

They met Crassus, leading all of Rome's available legionaries south. Outnumbered and out-disciplined, the slaves fought bravely, but were defeated. Spartacus was killed in the battle, and six thousand of his followers were crucified along the road to Rome.

General Pompey came rushing back from his victory in Spain, just in time to cut down the few escaping fugitives of Spartacus' army. He then managed to arrive in Rome before Crassus and was awarded a full-scale triumph; the furious Crassus had to be content with a more modest victory parade.

This Pompey – known as "the Great" after an earlier victory in Africa – was a soldier cast in the same mould as Marius and Sulla: a formidable general (with more than a touch of vainglory) but a less than brilliant politician. Two years after his "victory" over Spartacus, he stood for consul; when the patricians rejected him as legally too young (he was thirty-six) he changed sides and joined the people's party, of which Crassus was a leading light.

During the war with Spartacus, the pirates had become bolder than ever and the Romans were becoming absolutely desperate. With most of their corn being intercepted, Roman plebeians were starving on the streets. Coastal towns had been raided and sacked so many times that the survivors had simply moved inland permanently – further damaging sea trade. The pirates landed where they pleased, and often roamed around until they found someone who was worth kidnapping for ransom. And paying such ransoms was becoming an all too regular part of patrician family life. The Romans felt a terrible sense of helplessness: there were so many pirate vessels all over the Mediterranean, and the strongest army could do nothing against them.

In 68 BC., Pompey and his supporters persuaded the people of Rome that something had to be done, even if it cost millions of gold pieces. The following year, Pompey raised 120,000 men and 270 ships. He knew which towns were pirate strongholds, it was just a matter of attacking them all at once so that the pirates could not co-operate or reinforce one another. He had been given three years to complete his task. He struck so suddenly and violently that he completed half of it in the first forty days.

The Romans were poor seamen, but it turned out that this made no difference. The pirates fled into their strongholds as soon as the Romans appeared on the horizon, and then Roman soldiers poured on shore and smoked them out. These murderers and robbers were no match for trained Roman legions; and when the word got around that Pompey would be merciful to all who surrendered, they gave up by the thousand.

Mithridates of Pontus – Sulla's old adversary – who had supported the pirates of Cilicia, watched in dismay as the strongholds crumbled. Twenty thousand pirates were captured, ten thousand killed, and all their strongholds and shipyards destroyed. Then, instead of crucifying his captives, Pompey resettled them in some of the abandoned towns, knowing that most of them would settle down to earning a respectable living when given the chance. He proved to be correct. In just three months, Pompey put an end to Mediterranean piracy for many generations to come.

After this triumph the Roman people were convinced that Pompey was irresistible, so they sent him with an army to Asia Minor to finish off Mithridates, who was now being more trouble-some than ever – encouraging his son-in-law Tigranes to annex

Dictators

Syria and Cappadocia. Pompey captured Tigranes, and pursued Mithridates to the Crimea, where the latter committed suicide on hearing that his own son had joined Rome against him.

The Senate had awarded Pompey the right to declare war in the name of Rome, without seeking their permission first – as long as he was away from Rome, they were happy to grant him kingly authority. He used his unprecedented power to good effect. When the rulers of Judaea, the Maccabees, asked Pompey to send troops to sort out an internal dispute within the country, he agreed with alacrity. He then crushed both feuding parties and declared the land of the Jews a Roman province. It was a trick that Rome would later use to capture first Egypt, then Britain. Apparently unstoppable, Pompey then went on to march as far as the Caspian Sea. His achievement was as remarkable, in its way, as that of Alexander the Great. Meanwhile an ally of Pompey, Julius Caesar, was making a name for himself, expanding Roman control of Spain. This Caesar was a remarkable young man, a nephew of Marius, whose talents had been so obvious when he was in his early twenties that it was only with difficulty that the dictator Sulla was dissuaded from having him killed. Like his uncle Marius, Caesar dreamed of glory and triumph, but no one expected him to become a great national leader. As a youth he had been fashionably foppish, writing poetry, perfuming and curling his hair and having numerous love affairs – with men as well as women. His fellow Romans regarded him much as Oscar Wilde was by Londoners in the 1890s – a clever socialite, but not likely to achieve high office. Mommsen, the great German nineteenth century historian, described Caesar as "Rome's sole creative genius" but, like most Romans, Caesar lacked the imagination to be genuinely creative. For all his artistic pretensions, Caesar was a warlord at heart.

For example, he possessed a good measure of the Roman ruthlessness. As a young man, he had been captured by pirates, who had told him they wanted twenty talents (a Greek measure for large amounts of gold) in ransom; Caesar said haughtily that they were insulting him and he would give them fifty talents.

Waiting for the ransom to arrive, he lived among them as if they were his servants, telling them to be quiet when he wanted to sleep. He joined in their games and made them sit and listen while he read them his poetry; when they proved less than appreciative, he called them barbarians and told them he would have them crucified when he was freed. They laughed indulgently at the spoilt and imperious young man.

As soon as the ransom arrived and the pirates let him go, Caesar hurried to the nearest port – Miletus in Asia Minor – commandeered several ships and returned to surprise them. As he had promised, he had them all crucified but, as a humane concession, cut their throats before nailing them to the crosses.

Back from his minor victories in Spain, Caesar was appointed as the *Adile*: the master of ceremonies in public celebrations. This seems to have underlined the Senate's opinion of him as a fop and a political lightweight, but Caesar put the posting to good use. He borrowed large sums from Crassus and staged some spectacular shows, one of them with 320 pairs of gladiators. This quickly made Caesar immensely popular with the plebeians – which is why Crassus was willing to bankroll his young friend almost without limit.

When Pompey came back from his conquests in 62 BC, Julius Caesar was becoming a power to be reckoned with, while the patrician Senate showed its jealousy of Pompey by snubbing him (after all, he *had* gone over to the people's party, and his unilateral power to declare wars naturally did not affect Rome itself). Caesar suggested an alliance: he was the most popular man in Rome, Crassus was the richest, Pompey was its greatest hero; together they could do what they liked. This oddly assorted trio – the egotistical general, the ambitious millionaire and the still rather foppish intellectual – entered into a partnership that would make them masters of Rome. Theoretically the Senate could be overruled by the people, if the plebeian leaders spoke with one voice – an event so rare that the Senate had never made any real attempt to strengthen their position against the people's party. Ever since the unfortunate affair of the triumph over Spartacus, Pompey and Crassus had been rivals. Now they both saw the virtue of the alliance, and put their grievances aside. The three became known to their friends as "the triumvirate", to their enemies as "the three-headed monster."

If the Senate initially thought the triumvirate was just another petty alliance – the sort of thing that constantly grew up and collapsed in the volatile world of Roman politics – they badly misjudged the "monster". Caesar's political savvy, married to Pompey's reputation and military discipline, all backed by Crassus' millions, made the three men the most powerful force the Senate had faced since Sulla. And the triumvirate had no intention of ever retiring and "returning to the plough" as Sulla had.

In the following year, 59 BC, the three-headed monster achieved the first of its aims: Caesar was elected consul, in the teeth of bitter opposition from the patricians. His co-consul, a hardline patrician, was so disgusted at Caesar's election, he refused to perform his duties – thus playing into the triumvirate's hands and leaving Caesar to effectively preside as sole consul. Caesar then used his power to get Pompey what he most wanted: land for his retiring soldiers. Then Pompey and Crassus were appointed head of a commission to administer new laws – a position that allowed them to target their enemies with selective legislation. Thus the three men became the rulers of Rome in all but name.

It could have been the beginning of a new era. All three men were intelligent. None of them had the temperament of a tyrant. Together they could have steered the whole country into a new age of prosperity and enlightenment. But somehow Rome was not destined to become a new Athens. It had gone too far down the road to empire.

Caesar soon became tired of the endless back-biting and in-fighting in the Senate, and marched off to Gaul (France) looking for adventure and glory. He found both over the next five years as his army, in a stunning series of battles, subdued the Gauls from the Rhine to the North Sea, then crossed the English Channel and defeated the southern Britons. This might not seem much compared to Pompey's victories over more civilized peoples in the Middle East, but the Romans knew better. The Gaulish warriors, and their British cousins, were some of most feared fighters in the known world. Their brief invasion of Italy in 390 BC had left the nightmare memory of giant, blond-haired warriors – most were over six feet high, while the Romans rarely topped five foot ten – who fought with a savage fearlessness, even when badly wounded. The Gauls were the Vikings of Caesar's day. Yet, with a single military force against the whole Gaulish nation, Caesar had won a total victory, forever removing the fear of invasion of Italy from the north-west frontier.

Back in Rome, Pompey and Crassus viewed these triumphs with mixed feelings. The three-headed monster could only remain stable as long as none of the heads got too big. Caesar was clearly getting too powerful. Crassus, determined to win the full triumph Pompey had once robbed him of, got himself appointed to the command of the Roman army in Syria and went off to try to outdo Caesar by invading Parthia (now Iran). The campaign proved to be a disaster. Fighting trained Parthian troops rather than rebellious slaves, Crassus badly misjudged the situation. Roman foot soldiers were the best in the world, but the Roman cavalry was weak. In contrast, the Parthian mounted archer was the best cavalryman the world would see until the advent of Genghis Khan's Mongol Horde. Sweltering in heavy armour beneath the desert sun, Roman legionaries could not deal with an enemy that fired volleys of arrows, then rode away before they could be counterattacked. Crassus' army was hit-and-run to death and he was captured and executed. Legend has it that, as an ironic compliment to Crassus' vast fortune, his mouth was filled with molten gold.

On hearing the news, and seeing that now was their chance to break the plebeian party stranglehold on government, the patricians offered to make Pompey sole consul of Rome. Pompey was now getting old, and must have feared that he could not handle Caesar without Crassus to balance matters. He decided to betray his political partner and changed sides from the plebeian to the patrician party. Caesar was ordered to leave his army and return to Rome.

Despite all he had done for the Republic, Caesar knew just how fickle the Roman mob was and just how vindictive the patrician Senate could be: if he returned to Rome without an army to protect him, he would be dead within days. He decided to disobey orders and marched his army to the banks of the river that divided Gaul from Italy – the Rubicon. There he waited, hoping that matters might still be smoothed over. But when Pompey and the Senate threw down the gauntlet, ordering him to disband his army or be considered a public enemy, Caesar gave the order to cross. It meant civil war.

The Rise of Caesar

While Pompey and his army withdrew to Greece to prepare for the coming battle, Caesar entered Rome in triumph and had himself reappointed sole consul by what remained of the Senate – naturally, all his most implacable enemies had left in a hurry. He then pacified the rest of Italy. The Roman armies of Spain had sided with their old commander, Pompey, so Caesar defeated them before turning to the greatest task. In Greece, Caesar defeated Pompey's vastly superior forces at the Battle of Pharsalus. Pompey escaped to Egypt and, as he stepped ashore, was stabbed in the back by his Egyptian hosts. Egypt was not interested in defeated generals, even ones as legendary as Pompey the Great.

Unaware that Pompey was dead, Caesar followed him to Egypt and found himself embroiled in a family squabble between the boy king Ptolemy and his teenage sister, Cleopatra. Caesar took Cleopatra's part – fathering a son on her – and defeated Ptolemy's army, with some help from the son of Rome's old enemy Mithridates. Cleopatra was installed on the throne of Egypt, as a Roman puppet, and Caesar sailed back to Rome to a magnificent public triumph – the leading chariot bore the words *Veni, vidi, vici*: "I came, I saw, I conquered." The Senate voted him the title of dictator; a post that few imagined he would ever give up voluntarily.

The civil war was not yet over, however. Caesar had a remaining enemy in the field, over whom it was important that he not only triumph, but also to whom he *must* show mercy: Marcus Porcius Cato, great-grandson of Cato the Censor (the man who had insisted on the ruthless destruction of Carthage in the previous century).

Cato was the unofficial leader of the patrician party but, unlike most of those he led, he was a model of old-world values. He lived frugally, wore simple black clothing instead of expensive fashion wear, and made a point of denouncing liberality and vice (Caesar's main character traits when not at war). There remains some debate over whether Cato was actually a down-to-earth puritan, or was simply a better fraud than his debauched fellow senators, but there is no doubt that he represented an ideal that Romans found viscerally attractive (provided they didn't have to follow it too closely themselves).

If Cato were killed, Caesar's standing as a republican first-among-equals would be badly damaged. If, on the other hand, he pardoned and – better still – became reconciled with the living embodiment of all that Rome liked to think it stood for, Caesar would gain considerable political kudos.

After separating from his ally Pompey, Cato's armies were driven out of Italy to North Africa. There they waited ineffectually while Pompey was destroyed and Caesar had his little adventure in Egypt. Their final stand against Caesar was at Thapsus – ironically, only a few miles from the scorched and cursed remains of Carthage.

Caesar won the battle with characteristic skill, and Cato made his way to the nearby fortress of Utica. There Cato held out until he was sure that Caesar was not pursuing the escaping remnants of his defeated army, then he stabbed himself in the stomach. When doctors tried to save him, Cato pushed them away and ensured his death by pulling his own guts out. For the Romans, who had little stigma against suicide, Cato died a truly noble death.

Dictators

Standing over Cato's corpse, Caesar said: "You envied me the pardon I would have given you, and I envy you your death."

It is tempting to think that Caesar might have foreseen his own ignoble death at that moment. Pompey had been just another would-be permanent dictator – Rome had had little to choose between him and Caesar. Cato, on the other hand, had never publicly sought power for power's sake; he was, in many ways, Caesar's reversed image. If Caesar could have used his considerable charms to win the defeated Cato over, they might have gone a long way to heal the rifts created by the civil war. Standing over Cato's body, Caesar probably realized that such a national reconciliation was now out of reach, and he himself would never be fully free from the risk of assassination.

Caesar was now sixty-five years old and was becoming increasingly imperious and distant in his manner. Many feared that the once fun-loving dandy was developing delusions of grandeur or even kingship, but it is also possible that, denied his reconciliation with Cato, Caesar was trying to emulate the old puritan. Yet, if he himself was cold, most of his works as Dictator of Rome were generous and reforming. He changed the calendar to fix the yearly slippage of a few hours that meant that the mid-summer festival was slowly edging into autumn. He rebuilt Carthage and settled new towns with his battle-weary ex-soldiers, giving each a generous grant of land. He extended Roman citizenship to what had previously been barbarian lands, such as areas of southern Gaul and, to represent these new citizens, he expanded the number of seats in the Roman Senate, diluting the power of the old patrician families.

This last, of course, did not go down well with the patrician party. If Caesar had been another Sulla, such angry grumbling and plotting would have been quickly dealt with by the executioner's sword, but Caesar set a deliberate policy of forgiving his enemies rather than beheading them. This was not an evidence of particular humanity on Caesar's part. He had ruthlessly ordered atrocities to be committed during his war with the Gauls but, despite the death of Cato, Caesar clearly meant to try to smooth over the ruptures of the civil war and, perhaps, he had developed an aversion to spilling more Roman blood.

The New Triumvirate

Caesar's growing unpopularity brought consequences. Less than a year after the death of Cato, a conspiracy grew up, spear-headed by former enemies of Caesar, but also backed by those he considered allies and friends. On the morning of 15 March 44 BC, Julius Caesar was stabbed to death during a visit to the Pompey Theatre. He had no bodyguards, and his friends did nothing to help him, but he initially fought off his twenty-three attackers until, seeing one called Decimus Brutus stab at him, he exclaimed "*Et tu, Brute*?" and, throwing a fold of his robe over his face, allowed them to kill him. Brutus was a particular favourite of Caesar's, being the son of Sevilia, a former lover, and history has remained muddied over Caesar's last words. Most historians believe he exclaimed "You too, Brutus?" but the Roman historian Suetonius reported that he actually cried: "You too, my son?"

Much has been made, by Shakespeare and others, of the supposedly noble aims of the conspirators – that Caesar hoped to make himself a king, and they wanted to defend democratic republican freedoms. But the fact is that Caesar had all the power he needed as "Dictator for Life" (a position awarded him by the Senate only a month before he was killed) and he had no legitimate children to past a hereditary monarchy on to.

In fact, it is hard not to believe that most of the conspirators struck at Caesar out of the petty vindictiveness that had come to typify the Republic's ruling class. His murder did not save the Republic, as they claimed it would, but plunged it into thirteen more years of brutal civil war that Rome barely survived. The assassination also martyred Caesar. If he had died in battle or, like Sulla, in his bed, the Republic might have continued – rotten to the core as it was. The killing in the Pompey Theatre ultimately sanctified Caesar's memory (literally – he was later voted to be a demigod by the Senate) and cleared the way for a new type of Roman dictator: the Emperor.

Caesar's nephew, Octavianus, emerged from the civil war as part of a new triumvirate. His co-dictators were the brilliant but dissolute general Mark Antony and a weakling patrician called Lepidus. However, this was not the relatively peaceable "three-headed monster" of Crassus, Pompey and Caesar's time – the endless civil wars had brutalized the victors and convinced them that the acquisition of absolute power was the only way to remain safe. Lepidus was quickly sidetracked and later imprisoned, and Octavianus and Mark Antony were soon squaring up for another civil war. By the end, Mark Antony and his lover, Queen Cleopatra, were dead and Octavianus was sole dictator of the Roman Republic.

But the Republic was now just a word and the Senate little better than a rubber stamp: real power rested in one man alone. Octavianus emphasized the transformation of the state by changing his name to the grander "Augustus" and the title of dictator to "emperor" (Latin for "supreme commander"). He continued to pretend that this office was temporary, but in his will he made sure that he named his successor to the emperorship – his stepson Tiberius. Rome, whatever it told itself, had a hereditary monarchy once again.

As we will see in the chapter on the Emperor Caligula some Roman emperors truly plumbed the depths of depravity. Others, like the peace-loving Vespasian and emperor-philosopher Marcus Aurelius, were as good as the times let them be. But the Punic curse – Rome's addiction to thinly justified violence and wars – meant that the Roman Empire remained forever in conflict, both externally with their neighbours and internally as patricians and military commanders endlessly plotted, assassinated and started civil wars to seize the throne. And the idea of the dictator – the ruthless thug who holds on to absolute power through violence and fear – was Rome's most emblematic legacy to the world.

Chapter One

Papa Doc:
Voodoo Gangster

In the late Summer of 1963, fifty badly trained soldiers, a motley bunch of exiles and dissidents, straggled through the humid, mountainous sub-tropical forest that spans the border between Haiti and the Dominican Republic. This pathetic army, weighed down by the CIA-supplied weapons it barely knew how to fire, was supposed to constitute a force capable of liberating Haiti from the regime of Doctor François Duvalier, better known as Papa Doc. It was the fourth such sad little invasion, and got as far as the others. Outnumbered and shot to pieces at its first encounter with Duvalier's forces, the expedition might simply have been another tragi-comic episode in Haiti's sorrowful history, were it not for the frightening postscript. One of the dead invaders was a Captain Blucher Philogenes, a former officer in Duvalier's army, who had frequently boasted that he was immune to bullets. On the specific orders of Duvalier, a Lieutenant Albert Jerome cut the head off the corpse. Packed in ice, it was delivered by a specially arranged airlift to the Palace. A weird rumour began to spread. In the still of the night, they said, Papa Doc would sit, staring desperately into the cold, lifeless eyes of his dead enemy, trying to learn what those still living planned.

There are many bizarre stories from Haiti, which has obstinately remained a cradle of witchcraft and superstition in the age of science. Duvalier was notorious for his use of Voodoo to manipulate the fears of his people. But this is not only the story of a mysterious bogeyman who wove a net of spells over Haiti. This is the story of a man who triumphed by doing nothing; who in fifteen years of absolute rule over a country, achieved absolutely nothing except the further abasement of an already degraded people; whose promises meant nothing, and who left nothing behind except terror. Most dictators at least manage to build a row of public toilets. More galling even than the sheer misery of the people is that this incompetent tyranny was sponsored to the tune of hundreds of millions of dollars in aid blackmailed from the American Government, eighty per cent of which went straight into the pockets of the foul brood in charge. As the International Commission of Justice said in words which barely concealed their incredulous shock at the blatant criminality:

> In today's world there are many authoritarian regimes. Generally speaking they are the reflection of some ideology. The tyranny that oppresses Haiti does not even have that excuse; its sole object is to place the country under tribute in order to ensure the future affluence of those now in power.

Haiti has never been served well by its rulers, white or black, who have traditionally acquired power by violence and are obliged to maintain it with fear. Barely five minutes of its strange and violent history have been devoted to the welfare of the population rather than the enrichment of the powerful. The best the people could hope for in the 1957 elections was a benign criminal who might allow them a few crumbs off his table. In the unassuming, bespectacled and soft-spoken Dr François Duvalier, they found an outright gangster. They had always given their rulers names, but Duvalier did not even give them that privilege. He christened himself "Papa Doc", and in a clear sign of what was to come announced:

> As President I have no enemies and can have none. There are only enemies of the nation . . .

The implication was terrifying. He was the people; they had no voice other than him, and he considered every murder to be sanctioned by them. They were his property, and he would end up selling their own blood to keep his pockets full.

Duvalier had campaigned as the saviour of the masses, the wretched black peasants who had suffered at the hands of its mulatto elite since Haiti became the first, black independent State in 1804. Over ninety per cent of the population were illiterate, most earning the equivalent of £1 per week or less, and few having an average life expectancy over thirty-five. Papa Doc was a champion of traditional Haitian culture, and stressed the importance of this as a means to creating a nation with an identity. He was an acutely vain man, who considered himself an exceptional intellectual. The only clarity in his speeches came when he praised himself. Otherwise they were incomprehensible goobledegook, stuffed full of confused mystic twittering. Two crucial influences he had often paraded were the idea of "negritude" and, of course, the ancient folk religion of Haiti, Voodoo.

To understand these better, it is helpful to know a little of Haiti's remarkable history.

Haiti shares the Caribbean island of Hispaniola with the Dominican Republic. It is a lush but wild country, which was once the single richest colony on earth. The island was initially conquered by the Spanish, who within eighteen years of Columbus' discovery of America, had worked the native population of Arawak Indians to death, in their search for gold. The Spanish also bequeathed a variety of European diseases to the Indians, which killed off those they had overlooked.

After a period as a haven to pirates, the island came under French control as an affluent plantation worked by slaves imported from West Africa. The Africans brought their tribal customs and gods with them. Christianity had little impact. The teachings of the Catholic missionaries, full of rituals, resurrection, saints and hell were simply absorbed into their folk beliefs to create the heady brew that is Voodoo. In Voodoo, the Catholic creed, the Apostles creed and the Hail Mary are all used in the ceremonies. The Virgin Mary appears as Grande Erzulie, Goddess of Fertility. The Cross of Christ is a symbol of Baron Samedi, lord of the dead. Saint Peter is Papa Legba. God exists, but he is aloof, remote and indifferent. Those who practise Voodoo are appealing to the lesser spirits or "loas" to help them with the daily requirements of life – food, sex, shelter, disease and protection from enemies – when no other power on earth will. There are two types of these spirits: "Rada" which are African, and "Petro", which are particularly Haitian and much more violent and unpredictable. Voodoo priests are known as "Houngans". Papa Doc became a houngan early on in his evolution. In addition there are sorcerers called "bocors" who specialize in practising the magic that is part of the religion. They cast the spells and curses, the "ouanga". The peasant's biggest moment is death. He may mortgage and sell all that he possesses to ensure a proper funeral, when his personal god will be removed from his body and return to mystical Guinea. The houngan will be well paid to ensure that his corpse does not become the zombie slave of an enemy.

Duvalier employed both priests and sorcerers to scan the future, and used his personal influence over the hundreds of local bocors to maintain his hold on the people of the most remote regions. He moved from practising Voodoo to dabbling in black magic. Contrary to popular belief, Voodoo does not normally do deals with the devil. Reputable houngans reject "magie noire"; they know that in order to practise it one must make a bargain with evil spirits and ultimately be destroyed.

The first slave rebellions of 1791 began in an atmosphere of tropical storms and night-time voodoo sacrifices; the first slave leader was a famed Voodoo priest, a giant, called Brookman. It was under Toussaint Louverture that the slaves gained their freedom, only to lose it when Napoleon sent 43,000 troops to restore slavery. The French imported dog: from Cuba which they trained to pursue and kill the blacks, but even this unspeakable cruelty could not stem the tide. Dessalines, the great Haitian hero whom Papa Doc was so fond of comparing himself to, so thrashed the French that they surrendered to the British rather than face the fury of his ragged army. When Boisrond Tonnere, one of Dessalines' officers, came to write the Act of Independence in 1804, he famously said:

> To write this Act of Independence we must have a white man's skin for parchment, his skull for an inkwell, his blood for ink and a bayonet for a pen . . .

The violent racism of a world still dependent on slavery isolated Haiti which was an unwanted example of a free black nation. It was crippled by debt, and fell under the heel of a string of black tyrants. Between 1843 and 1915 alone, there were twenty-two dictators. Most were assassinated by their successors. The more educated mulatto elite, the half-breeds, with Negro mothers and white fathers tended to be born into more favourable circumstances and became the aristocracy, with the blacks an embittered majority. Hence, in the twentieth century, the evolution of the idea of "negritude" – the attempt to raise the pride and consciousness of the negro majority, who for so long had felt cursed by their colour. Unfortunately, under Duvalier this became an excuse to tell the people that only he knew what was good for them. He was never slow to play the race card to justify his atrocities or explain why his country was in a mess; it could always be blamed on the racism of another nation. On the advice of friends, Duvalier also married a mulatto.

François Duvalier was born in 1907 in a tin-roofed shack a few streets away from the National Palace. He was the son of a primary school teacher and a bakery employee. His early childhood was spent in an atmosphere of continuous revolution and tyranny, as the British, French, Germans and Americans played poker with Haiti, each underwriting their favoured dictators. After would-be Emperor Guillame Sam was impaled on the railings of the French Embassy, the US finally sent in the marines, who remained until 1934. Their occupation was widely resented, and there were frequent suicide bombings, but they left hospitals, telephones, bridges and schools.

Duvalier was a quiet, forgettable pupil during his early education and afterwards went on to medical school. He had become involved on the fringes of student politics and protests. Significantly, he fell under the influence of Lorimer Denis, a twenty-four-year-old Voodoo mystic and mainspring of the "Negritude" movement, and began to write for *Action National*, the nationalist newspaper. In his articles he criticized the US occupation, and praised the flowering of traditional Haitian culture hoping that "A man will come to correct injustice and set things right".

The moment the Marines went, the population went on an illogical orgy of destruction, tearing up the bridges and telephone systems their white rulers had left. It was this instinctive and irrational hatred that Duvalier was later able to harness. So strife-torn were the years that followed that in the words of one of Duvalier's associates, "François was the only one of his generation who never knew the inside of a prison." Duvalier kept his head down, and worked on his strategy of doing nothing which was later to serve him so well. He continued to dabble in "Haiti's traditional culture" and became a houngan or Voodoo priest by virtue of his knowledge. He also continued to write, under an assumed name, but was incapable of doing anything without the help of the Voodoo mystic, Denis. His articles vowed to restore the National pride of Haiti, and contained the same vain boast that he would repeat all his life: "We swear to make our motherland the Negro miracle." Duvalier worked in a series of government hospitals as a consultant, and in 1943 was chosen to work alongside some US doctors on a project intended to wipe out the terrible, contagious disease called "yaws" that afflicted over seventy per cent of the population. It was on the evidence of this association that the Americans later thought he might be a suitable candidate for their support.

From here, having done only what he was told, he made it,

without doing anything, to the position of Director of Public Health, where he did nothing. He had been fortunate that his self-styled reputation as an "intellectual" had secured him a prominent position in the new Nationalist party; his position in the Government came by default, when the current dictator failed to rig the elections sufficiently and was forced to buy the Nationalists' support in a coalition with a few ministerial goodies. Here, while all around him indulged in frenzied activity and disastrous blunders, Duvalier's revolutionary policy of doing nothing came into its own. It continued to be his most successful tactic, and ensured he kept his job, and eventually was promoted to Cabinet Minister for Public Health and Labour. As he never directly expressed a view, he made no enemies; and as he did nothing, there was no action he could be criticized for. It was ingenious.

Under Dumarsais Estime, who had won power with the support of the army, a new class of black elite, like Duvalier, began to emerge, breaking into business and government, and challenging the mulattos. Unfortunately, those obtaining power were no better to their fellow men, and displayed prodigious indiscipline and greed. The mulattos persuaded the army to round on their former ally and in 1950, Colonel Paul Magloire became the umpteenth dictator in Haiti's short history.

Duvalier's inexorable rise to the top was halted. Thwarted, he finally did something and left the Government before Magloire could devise an unpleasant end for him. He went back to treating yaws. He acquired a lasting distrust of the army, and was further embittered by the sight of new favourites overtaking him. His behaviour became paranoid and he took to constantly switching plates with his dinner companions to avoid poisoning.

Magloire had a reputation as a playboy. Haiti became a decadent and sexy international attraction. The international literati – Noel Coward, Truman Capote and Graham Greene – flocked to it. The lavish excesses of its leader and the lingering smell of corruption and violence stimulated the jaded appetites of the tourists that thronged to its capital, Port-Au-Prince. The Americans were already providing considerable financial support, but in return asked that Haiti should be maintained a Communist-free zone. Magloire was only too happy to oblige, and took it further by shooting anyone suspected of promoting unrest.

In 1954 Magloire lined up his sights on Duvalier, who spent the next couple of years in hiding, dressed as a woman. There was considerable political unrest in the country, and though Duvalier had done very little, if anything, to agitate, the Government needed an enemy to blame for the spreading dissent. Hence Duvalier, whose contribution to democracy had been to write a few half-baked articles, was built up into the big, bad wolf, and found himself acknowledged as the leader of the opposition. His enemies created him as a plausible leader. In 1956, he dropped his skirts and came out of hiding, disassociating himself from the continued killings and bombings. It was, predictably, nothing to do with him. Although by this time he was probably doing something, namely using Voodoo to frighten the peasants into economically ruining the Government, he had changed his tack. Before, he had done nothing. He was still true to those values, but now he told other people to do things, like bomb and shoot. He was still untarnished by action.

Magloire fled to Jamaica, and elections were called. Reporters frankly found Duvalier a bit odd. He was unable to answer their questions regarding what he stood for, preferring to offer them a bit of mystic philosophy here and there. The election campaign was a virtual civil war; there were six changes of leader in the course of it. In one incident, over 1,000 of Duvalier's opponents were massacred in Port-Au-Prince. The results were a final proof of his magical powers; in some areas his vote alone was double the entire population. Such popularity is traditional among Haitian dictators.

The elections also marked the death of Duvalier's longtime guru, Lorimer Denis. People whispered that Duvalier had given his friend to the Voodoo spirits in order to ensure his election as President.

There were two priorities facing the new President of Haiti: firstly to guarantee that he was well paid for the job, and secondly, that he could keep it. The people thought that the President's chair had an evil spell over it. His solution to both was to turn to America.

The key was Communism. Cuba was shortly to fall to Castro, and Duvalier was quick to exploit the US fear of Communism spreading through the Caribbean: "Communism has established centres of infection – no area in the world is as vital to American security as the Caribbean . . ." he reminded the US, adding that he hoped Haiti could become the "spoiled child" of America.

For the next fifteen years he continued to flirt with Communism to keep the dollars coming. By 1960, quite apart from the vast loans he had extorted, the US had given Duvalier $22 million. In addition, on his election he had promised Cuba's dictator, Batista, that he would, for a price, not help Castro's Communist rebels. Batista's henchmen got a million dollar kickback for arranging the deal, Duvalier personally got $3 million, and Haiti got the few cents left over. The President was off to a flying start. After Cuba became Communist he had the Americans over a barrel. His country didn't need any industry when he could make millions of dollars from doing nothing. The Duvalier philosophy began to pay off.

Loans were received from the US for educational and health projects and the little that was left after everybody had taken their cut was wasted on grandiose plans – hotels and jet airports, which were never finished. Over fifty per cent of the country's entire budget came from the US, and American experts estimated that Duvalier's personal income could have funded a comprehensive aid programme for the entire nation. Within a few years of his election, the annual bill for his personal security amounted to a staggering $28 million, half of the country's yearly expenditure. His Secret Police, the Ton Ton Macoute, cost another $15 million.

Dictators

He resented any notion that the US should supervise the funds it gave to Haiti, and encouraged left-wing, student disturbances to give the Americans the jitters. He even dressed his troops up to look like Castro's gaily coloured revolutionaries. The Cuban Missile Crisis, when the Americans discovered that Russia was building missile launching sites on Cuban soil, within spitting distance of Florida, played straight into his hands. After deliberating, he came out in support of the US who were forced to keep paying him. When President Kennedy cut off aid he threatened to "bring him to his knees", and reputedly put a "ouanga" on him. Weirdly enough, Kennedy was shot shortly afterwards.

All this may falsely give the impression that he was doing something. In reality, he still did absolutely nothing but had discovered that he only had to imply that he might in the future do something, like vote Communist, and everybody paid him to stay completely still.

The magazine, *Newsweek*, described him as "Big Brother masquerading as the Mad Hatter", a reference to the dark suits and top hats he took to wearing and said:

> He moves hyperslowly, speaks in a whisper; his eyelids droop. Wearing a slightly bemused unshakeable half-smile, he does nothing for disconcertingly long periods of time and Haitian people, susceptible to the unusual, are awed . . .

He improved his absolute stillness by taking increasingly large doses of Voodoo, consulting the entrails of goats and speaking to the Gods as he sat in his bathtub wearing a top hat. "Haitian democracy is defined and refined as a national discipline within the revolution," he gibbered to passing journalists.

America provided the major part of his income. The rest had to be extracted from people by less glamorous means. He put this in the capable hands of Clement Barbot, under whom evolved the Ton Ton Macoute, the Secret Police force. An old Haitian tale features a giant bogeyman who strides from mountain to mountain stuffing little boys and girls into his knapsack or "macoute". Hence he is called Uncle Knapsack, or Ton Ton Macoute. These human bogeymen had a uniform of dark glasses and machine guns. There were up to 10,000 of them, unrestrained by any law. Technically, any Government employee could join; extortion was a civil service perk.

The Government's potential sources of revenue were the sale of gambling and hotel concessions, and monopolies on everything from sugar and cement to matches. Each time these changed hands vast amounts of money fell into the pockets of Duvalier and Barbot. Within a few months, Barbot had sold and resold the gambling concession three times, even though it was still owned by an Italian. Barbot was a chillingly efficient henchman, but was arrested and imprisoned when he yet again sold the gambling concession, and didn't cut Duvalier in on the deal. He told the purchasers that Papa Doc needed the money to build a hospital.

Barbot, a thoroughly evil man in his own right, later escaped and became Duvalier's most hated enemy. He told the *Washington Post* that Duvalier had informed him that he, personally, wished to kill three hundred people a year. The peasants of Haiti said that Barbot too had magical powers, and could assume the shape of a black dog at will. Duvalier panicked and ordered all black dogs to be shot on sight.

His successor as favourite was Luckner Cambronne, a bright young man who declared that "a good Duvalierist stands ready to kill his children, or children kill their parents". No-one ever defined Duvalierism better.

Cambronne was charged with raising funds for Papa Doc's pet project, Duvalierville, a new town to commemorate his greatness. Cambronne set about his task with zeal, using every means imaginable, including tolls, threats, beatings and torture. Even schoolchildren were mugged for donations to "The National Renovation Fund", a bottomless pit from which the money poured into the private bank accounts of officials. Cambronne had one inspired idea for fund raising. Thousands

Dictators

> "Duvalier has performed an economic miracle. He has taught us to live without money and eat without food. Duvalier has taught us how to live without life . . ."

of people received extortionate bills for using telephones that had never worked or, in some cases, had never been installed. Cambronne explained that, when all the bills were paid, the telephone service would be restored to working order.

Duvalierville was supposed to be finished in six months. At the end, there was only a pile of rubble and a sign swinging in the wind, the name already fading.

Tourism, another vital source of income, plummeted by seventy per cent. Duvalier launched a $40,000 drive to bring the tourists back. Typically, he ruined it by simultaneously stringing up the decomposing body of one of his opponents opposite the "Welcome to Haiti" sign at the airport. Poverty and despair were joint kings of Haiti.

When aid and hard currency became hard to obtain, he compelled peasants to donate blood in exchange for a few days' wages. This was then sold in America for $20 a litre.

To keep power, he again enlisted the help of the Americans. Because of the previous occupation, the mere sight of a marine was enough to send the Haitians screaming into the under-growth. They regarded the Americans with superstitious terror. Duvalier persuaded the Americans to send a small unit of marines over to train his own forces. Once they were there, he clung on to them. Their presence, however neutral, gave his regime an almost divine authority.

Opposition was outlawed. A state of emergency was declared, with a permanent curfew. The homes of potential opponents were bombed. He could have no enemies, and so he told the world's press that there were only two political prisoners in Haiti and one was a friend of his.

Jacques Alexis, Haiti's foremost novelist and a committed

Communist, had once been a hero of Duvalier's. He was now an obstruction to the inevitable progress of Duvalierism. He was accused of being behind the left-wing unrest which Duvalier himself had encouraged. Alexis left Haiti to attend a conference. Forbidden to return, he tried to slip in over the border but was caught by the Ton Ton Macoute. Under their encouragement, the peasants and children, the very people he had fought for, tore out his eyes and stoned him to death.

Under pressure from the US Duvalier held a "sneak" election in 1961, after which he declared himself President for another six years, because irrespective of whose name the people chose to write on their ballot papers, his name appeared on every one. This was true; the ballot papers issued to voters had his name printed at the bottom. He told the people: "I am and I symbolize an historic moment in your history as a free and independent people. God and the people are the source of all power. I have taken it, and damn it, I will keep it forever . . ."

He helpfully explained his success as a divine sign: "I am already an immaterial being." He had a very royal habit of addressing himself in the third person, as if talking about a disembodied, holy spirit. ". . . this giant capable of eclipsing the sun because the people have already consecrated me for life . . ."

At the next election he was the only candidate, and he thereafter regarded elections as an unnecessary activity, and declared himself President for life. Finally he changed the Constitution to ensure the dynastic succession of his equally loathsome son, Baby Doc.

He split his time between practising Voodoo and writing tributes to himself for the press to print: "Duvalier is the professor of energy, electrifier of souls . . . powerful multiplier of energy . . . renovator of Haitian Fatherland . . . synthesizes all there is of courage, bravery, genius, diplomacy, patriotism and tact . . ."

Whatever this homicidal fruitcake was taking, it was fairly potent. His reputed use of Voodoo was the strongest means to maintain a hold over Haiti. Catholic priests were persecuted and

> "Some people get crazy. They are not responsible for their actions and anyway, I am a doctor . . ."

expelled. The Vatican excommunicated the Haitian authorities. In response, Duvalier's Militia chief held a Voodoo ceremony on the steps of the Cathedral, smearing them with pigs' blood. The funeral procession of Clement Joumelle, a prominent opponent, was hijacked by the Ton Ton Macoute, who drove off with the body and refused to let a Catholic priest bless the interment. It transpired that Joumelle's heart had been removed to make a powerful "ouanga". There were stories of Duvalier burying people alive at the foot of a giant cross in the Bel Air region of Haiti, and sacrificing babies, which had become plentiful and cheap in a nation so poverty stricken that mothers openly sold their children for forty cents.

The opposition dug up Duvalier's father and extracted his heart to put a spell on Papa Doc's powers, splattering human excrement over the corpse and tomb. It didn't work.

In spite of these blood-curdling events, the average Haitian is easygoing and abhors physical violence, venting their anger in highly coloured curses and threats which are rarely carried out. The violence of the few oppresses the many, who have such a bloody history that they are profoundly fatalistic and cynical about all governments, and tend to simply endure the latest horrors.

There were more orthodox, but equally bizarre attempts to dethrone Papa Doc. Shortly after he took power, a mere eight men rode into town, took the main barracks and narrowly failed to capture the Palace and President. This was the famous "Dade County Sheriff's Invasion", so called because the "army" included a couple of Florida deputy sheriffs. They did have reinforcements of sixteen in reserve, but these never made it from Miami. The Haitians were terrified of the white invaders,

He founded the "Praise Papa Doc" movement and published a staggering bit of self-flattery, called "Catechisms of the Revolution", a parody of the Catholic prayer book with himself as the Holy Trinity. The Lord's Prayer began:

"Our Doc, who art in the National Palace for life, hallowed be thy name by present and future generation. Thy will be done in Port-Au-Prince and in the Provinces . . ."

who found the defending forces armed with wooden sticks and broom handles; Duvalier didn't trust them to have guns, which most couldn't shoot anyway. It was a long time before the Haitians realized the size of the invading force. Even so, it took all the available troops to winkle them out. Afterwards, Duvalier, who had been frantically packing his bag, posed in full army uniform, helmet and gun as a triumphant warrior who had seen off an army of thousands. An "international conspiracy" had been defeated. It transpired that the mercenaries were only going to receive $2,000 apiece. Some had invested their own savings in the invasion.

The US, which desperately hoped Duvalier would simply be overthrown, ended up supporting his regime with aid, whilst the CIA tried to undermine him through supporting the sad little efforts of the rebels. Nothing worked.

His death in 1971, from diabetes and heart failure, did not spell the end of the misery for Haiti. Jean Claude "Baby Doc" Duvalier succeeded him. This witless youth, the only son among five children, enjoyed the nicknames at school of "Fat Potato" and "Baskethead". So thick was he that he compelled the teachers to stop publicizing his grades at school. He was terrified at the prospect of stepping into his father's shoes, took an overdose of valium and missed the funeral. He devoted his

Dictators

time to fast cars and sex, leaving Mama Doc to get on with the serious business of looting the country. He didn't miss out, however. By the time of his overthrow in 1986, he had diverted at least $120 million into his pockets. His wife had flowers flown in from Miami at $50,000 a shot. Her jewellery required a mobile vault. She was utterly loathed by the people.

Amidst popular unrest, the Duvalier clan finally left Haiti aboard as US Airforce plane, which dropped them off in France, which, along with Libya, is a trash-can for used dictators. They live in Parisian suburbs, or are tucked away on the right wing coast of the South. There, in fashionable restaurants, nightclubs and hotels, you may find any number of redundant tyrants, wandering around with suitcases stuffed full of swag. They are good news for French business. Baby Doc lives in Cannes, the wealthy sun-spot on the Riviera. He sits alone in restaurants, and at night drives his BMW pointlessly up and down the sea front. Every six weeks, his courier disappears and comes back with a car-load of cash, reputedly $100,000.

In 1991, Haiti's first ever truly democratically elected President, Father Jean-Bertrand Aristide, took office. Seven months later, this popular Roman Catholic priest was forced out of office and into exile by a military coup. He had threatened the accumulated privilege of the few. Over the next few years Aristide pressured the international community to oust the illegal government and, in 1994, his efforts paid off. A UN task force of 20,000 troops (mostly American) forced the dictatorship out and reinstated Aristide. He ruled until 1995 when the constitution forced him to stand down (he was not allowed to stand in consecutive elections). However, he saw to it that a close colleague, Rene Preval, got the presidential ticket. Then Aristide stood for and won the 2000 election – which the opposition boycotted, claiming massive corruption. Then, in 2004, Aristide was yoyo-ed out of power again by a popular uprising.

It is debatable whether Father Aristide became – as his opponents claimed – just as corrupt as Papa Doc. But it is undisputed that Haiti remains one of the most hopeless places on earth. Major floods and mudslides in recent years have killed many people, but it would be wrong to blame Mother Nature, or even global warming. Commercial logging deforested much of the mountainous country in recent decades, removing the natural barrier against floods. Papa Doc's greed still curses Haiti to misery and death.

Chapter Two

The Emperor Caligula: Blood and Poison

Whatever the public thought, the Roman Emperors were not particularly interested in the virtues of restraint. Caligula's predecessor Tiberius, in whose loving care he spent a large portion of his early life, went into semi-retirement on the island of Capri where he established a colony of vice that beggars description. A lecher's Disneyland supervised by a Minister for Pleasures, and staffed with the selected youth of both sexes, its features included wall-to-wall pornography and round-the-clock, highly theatrical debauchery throughout the surrounding countryside. Children dressed as nymphs and satyrs sported in the woods; boys, whom Tiberius had chosen as "minnows", stocked his swimming pool. Even babies had their uses. One wonders what *Hello* magazine would have made of it all. Caligula spent five years on Capri under the personal tuition of this old goat, whose clinical pursuit of excess was only to be outdone by the bestial behaviour of his pupil.

Caligula was born on 31 August AD 12. He was one of six children. Augustus, then in his seventies, was still ruling. He had pursued a fruitful policy of "first among equals" with the Senate, and under him the Roman Empire had expanded into a miracle of political and military engineering, extending from the French coast to Palestine and Syria, from Africa and Egypt to Spain and Belgium boasting over 6,000 miles of frontier.

Caligula can have barely known anyone to die of natural causes. His mother and her parents, sisters and brothers were banished, murdered or condemned for treachery or promiscuity. His father was poisoned, his brothers disgraced. His brother

The Emperor. *Hulton-Deutsch*

Dictators

Drusus had been starved to death in prison, trying frantically to prolong his life by eating the stuffing from his mattress. Parentless, the remaining children were shipped from one relative to another. Around about the age of seventeen, Caligula began to sleep with his sisters. Drusilla was the first and favourite. She was about fourteen at the time that they were discovered in bed together by his great-aunt Antonia. He later had the other two, Livilla and Agrippina. Caligula regarded this incest as an exceptional experience. Years afterwards as Emperor, he asked Parsiensus Crispus, one of Rome's best-known wits if he had enjoyed sex with his sisters. "Not yet . . ." came the tactful reply.

An evil shadow hung over his branches of the family tree. His character, which the Romans hoped would be influenced by his noble bloodline, was instead distilled from the poison of his upbringing. The final products of the Imperial stable were not thoroughbreds, but maggot-ridden corpses, with only the diseased and deranged surviving.

In AD 37 Tiberius finally died. In his final years he had appointed an ambitious outsider, named Macro, to the position of Captain of the guard. Macro was so desperate to ensure his future that he encouraged his wife to sleep with Caligula. It was Macro who helped Caligula to climb over the final corpses between him and the throne.

Tiberius fell seriously ill at Misenum on the Bay of Naples, not far from his beloved Capri. Macro rushed to join Caligula at his deathbed, and they removed the Imperial signet ring from Tiberius' finger. Long before he died, agents were dispatched to the outposts of the Empire to proclaim Caligula Emperor. They knew that Tiberius had made a will and that they must secure power before the contents became public. Tiberius nearly scuppered their plans by suddenly reviving and demanding his ring back, but Caligula and Macro ended his long goodbye, smothering him with his own bedclothes.

Life under Tiberius had been grey, grim and repressive. He had only been prevented from killing many more of his enemies by the influence of his popular astrologer Thrasyllus, who kept predicting a longer life for him, thus convincing him he could afford to take the murders steadily. This saved many people from certain death. Now the Romans wanted to celebrate. Only Caligula prevented them from throwing Tiberius' body into the Tiber. By the time his will was read, Caligula was already Emperor. The will actually named Caligula as joint heir along with another relative, Tiberius Gemellus. It was not a happy document for Gemellus, bequeathing him and his family only inevitable death at Caligula's hands.

In his opening speech Caligula promised co-operation and respect with the Senate, humbly casting himself as their junior. He had grown into a big, tall, balding man, with a thin neck, thin legs and thin hair. He had hollow eyes and temples, a bulbous nose and a withdrawn lower lip. He was not pretty. He had been epileptic as a boy, and was quarrelsome as an adult, and had become a haunted insomniac. The isolation and fear of his childhood had taught him the virtues of hypocrisy. He wept at Tiberius' funeral. Whatever madness and revenge he had in mind he kept it under control and devoted himself to restoring the memory of his tragic, ghostly family. A little later he would appease those unquiet ghosts with rivers of blood.

His mother had games and sacrifices in her honour. He made a pilgrimage to retrieve her ashes from exile and lay them beside Augustus. Coins had her image on them. He named the month of September after his father Germanicus. The laws that the Senate had passed against the descendants of Germanicus were rescinded. This had never happened before. Not content, he bestowed titles on all surviving members of his family, and had his sisters made honorary Vestal Virgins. They were even included in the oath of Imperial allegiance: "I shall not hold myself or my children dearer than I do Gaius Caligula and his sisters."

Declaring an end to the puritan days of Tiberius, Caligula welcomed back the political exiles. An end was promised to treason trials. The files on suspects, he said, had been destroyed.

Dictators

The games, banned by Tiberius, were re-staged in spectacular fashion by Caligula; the new Temple of the Divine Augustus was dedicated with the sacrifice of four hundred bears and lions apiece. Caligula threw money about in lavish style, giving each member of the Imperial guard the equivalent of a year's income. His behaviour was extravagant and emotional; he was very much the gay, generous public figure that the people wanted, inclined to grand spontaneous gestures which warmed the heart. Early on, he awarded an ex-slave 800,000 sesterces because he heard that she had refused to inform on her former employer, even under torture. The average income was about 1,000 sesterces so this made her a multi-millionaire. Perhaps Caligula was trying to tell the Romans that he thought loyalty was a rare quality among them.

In the words of Suetonius, "So much for the prince; now for the monster."

A few months into his reign he fell very ill and nearly died. During his illness, a prominent citizen, Publius Politus, tried to prove his love for Caligula by publicly vowing that he would willingly sacrifice his life to ensure the Emperor's recovery. Not to be outdone, another, Atanius Secundus, announced he would happily fight a gladiator. Recovering, Caligula generously gave them the opportunity to fulfil their hypocritical promises. Publius was dressed up in sacrificial garments and dragged through the streets by slaves, to be hurled off the Tarpeian Rock and into the Tiber. Atanius, who had never held a sword, got his fight, and to the death.

He began to interpret the most innocent behaviour as veiled treason. Silanus, the father of his dead wife, suffered from seasickness and politely declined to go on a boat-trip with Caligula, who divined from this that Silanus was hoping for a ship-wreck and instantly dispatched troops to murder him. In despair, Silanus slit his own wrists.

The unlucky Tiberius Gemellus, whom Tiberius had named as joint heir with Caligula, caught an unpleasant cold. In Caligula's presence, he treated himself with some cough medicine.

Caligula presumed this was an antidote to poison, which demonstrated that Gemellus distrusted him. "An antidote!" he said. "How can one take an antidote against Caesar?" In any case, he was sure that Gemellus had prayed for his death, and had both him and his family killed.

Macro, who had helped him to power, and been his constant companion, adviser and sycophant, went the way of all flesh, described by Caligula as ". . . the teacher of one who no longer needs to learn". As he had been sleeping with Macro's wife, he executed him for pimping.

During his illness Caligula had made Drusilla his heir. To make things more convenient, he freed her from her legal marriage and hitched her to a male lover of his, Marcus Lepidus, who became the heir-designate, though he was eventually executed for treason. Caligula was partial to both sexes. His sisters were his favourite women, but he liked others, particularly if they could be stolen. At a wedding he famously accused the bridegroom of "making love to my wife", and married the poor woman, Livia Orestilla, himself. He quickly divorced her and married Lollia Paulina, who was also the wife of another man. She lasted a few months. When he divorced her he forbade her to ever have sex again. With men, he adored the company of actors, and took several of the more famous ones as lovers, reflecting his childish addiction to the spectacle of the games and the theatre. An invitation to Caligula's bed could not be refused, and many happily dived in, looking for influence rather than pleasure. This was highly risky. He was fond of telling them that "you'll lose this beautiful head when I decide".

He had no concept of the value of money and it is hard to grasp the mountainous scale of his extravagance. Tiberius, miserly by nature, had left nearly three billion sesterces, the equivalent of six years' revenue, in the state coffers. Caligula got through it in a years', throwing it at favourites. He required daily amusement, and there were constant games, races and parties. He spent ten million sesterces, the annual tribute of three provinces, on a single dinner. The various kings deposed by Tiberius were restored, and their lost revenues returned to them. One received a hundred million sesterces, a quarter of the entire Empire's annual revenue.

These were the good times. In the Summer of AD 38, Drusilla died. Caligula was too distraught to attend her funeral, at which she was accorded the highest honours ever awarded to a woman. During a period of mourning he imposed on the city, Caligula made it a capital offence to laugh in public or private. Then he disappeared from Rome, returning with wild hair and eyes to demand that his dead sister be made a goddess. One quick-witted sycophant was given eight million sesterces for claiming he saw her ascend to heaven. The frightened Senate awarded her her own Shrines and priestesses and placed her golden image in the Senate house. It didn't avert the attentions of Caligula who told them that he had spoken to the ghost of Tiberius, who had told him: "Show no affection for them and spare none of them. For they all hate you and pray for your death, and they will murder you if they can."

Producing the secret files of Tiberius he claimed to have destroyed, he investigated the public trials of his family under Tiberius and discovered that the same senators who grovelled to him now had accused and passed sentence on his dead relatives.

The killings that followed had a richly theatrical flavour to them. Parents were forced to attend the execution of their children, and Caligula would sometimes invite them to dine with him afterwards. One senator, thrown to the lions, insisted on proclaiming his innocence. He was rescued, only for his tongue to be cut out before he was thrown back. Caligula had the limbs and bowels of another stacked in front of him. He favoured slow killings, ordering the executioner to "strike so that he may feel he is dying". The realization that he was running out of money gave added impetus to the endless treason trials. He increased his income by lopping off heads and confiscating estates. When one victim was discovered to have been bankrupt, Caligula regretfully said "he might just as well have lived". The money problem became particularly acute while he was on a trip to Lyon in Gaul. Informed that he had bankrupted the State, he sold off his Divine Sister's possessions. This proved so successful he had the contents of the Palace shipped from Rome, and proceeded to stage a series of auctions. The country's richest men were herded into these, where Caligula would compel them to buy family souvenirs at vastly inflated prices, introducing each item with a tag like "this belonged to my mother", or "Augustus got this from Antony". He was a brilliant auctioneer, and cunningly exploited the fear of his audience. Back in Rome, he auctioned off victorious gladiators to selected purchasers. One man, who dozed off for a few moments, woke to find he had purchased thirteen gladiators at a cost of nine million sesterces.

On another occasion in Lyon, when he was gambling and running low on cash he ordered the Public Census list of Gaul to be brought to him and selected a few wealthy men from the list of inhabitants. Ordering their deaths, he gleefully pointed out to his gambling companions that "while you play here for a few denarii, I have just made a hundred and fifty million".

The Senate was so terrified that it refused to meet, and when it did, spent all its time pathetically praising Caligula in the hope that he would spare them. "Let them hate me, so long as they fear me," he said. It wasn't simply the senators or those he imagined were treasonous or whose money he wanted that died, but now anyone that disappointed or irritated him faced torture and execution. The manager of the gladiatorial shows was beaten with chains for days. Caligula refused to kill him until he began to smell too bad. Writers were burned alive for ambiguity. He was only just waking up to the possibilities offered by absolute power. At a banquet one night, he suddenly burst out laughing and told his guests that he'd just realized he could have their heads removed at a single stroke.

But arbitrary murder was not a sufficient test of his authority, and his gestures became grander, as he strove for a confrontation with Heaven. Thrasyllus the favourite astrologer of Tiberius, had apparently told him that Caligula had as much chance of becoming Emperor as he had of riding on horseback across the Gulf of Baiae. Hearing this, Caligula ordered a bridge over three miles long to be built. Ships were anchored two abreast across the bay, and a road modelled on the Appian Way laid on top of them. So many ships were required that some had to be built, and the withdrawal of others from trade caused a financial catastrophe in Rome. In a two-day festival, Caligula charged pointlessly back and forth across the bridge at the head of a group of cavalry, dressed in the armour of Alexander the Great and crowned with jewels and oak-leaves. He gave a speech in which he praised himself for building this bridge and his troops for their courage in walking on water, and declared that the calmness of the sea indicated that the Gods themselves were now afraid of him.

Invasion and conquest were other ways he could express his Imperial powers. He hadn't quite made himself a god yet, but it was clearly on the cards. He dashed north into Germany, and tried to emulate his father's deeds by taking on the Huns. Unfortunately, he couldn't find any and was forced to send his own German bodyguards across the Rhine, so that the other troops could chase after them and bring them back as enemy captives. He hid Germans who were already prisoners in bushes and trees so that he could personally find them and force them to surrender. In moments of insecurity, he interrupted the hide-and-seek to call the Legions together and order them to Hail him Emperor.

Having subdued Germany, he now proceeded with the conquest of Britain. His unorthodox and peaceful invasion merits attention. He assembled his entire forces along the French coast, looking out across the Channel, facing the distant cliffs of Dover. Batteries of catapults and siege engines were lined up next to the troops. After an enormous wait, the troops began to embark onto ships, but were no sooner at sea than they were told to turn back. Caligula retreated to a tower, from which he demanded that a charge be sounded, and afterwards that the soldiers use their helmets and clothing to gather up seashells.

The Emperor Caligula: Blood and Poison

Wagon-loads of these, which he described as the spoils of his victory, were returned to Rome along with a few Gauls whom he dressed up and displayed as Germans and Britons.

There was nothing left for him to achieve as a mortal; he had done all that the public could expect of an Emperor. As everything was now permissible, the only way he could escape the terror of boredom was to elevate himself to godhead.

He built new quarters on the Capitoline Hill in order to be close to his "brother", Jupiter, whom he challenged to a duel when thunder interrupted a pantomime he was watching. A whole temple was dedicated to him, and he forced his family and senators to pay ten million sesterces each for the privilege of becoming his priests. He had always enjoyed dressing up as a woman; now he dressed himself as whatever deity took his fancy. He couldn't decide which god he was; he tried out all the male ones, and then appeared as Juno, Diana and Venus. Everybody had to prostrate themselves in his presence and the living grovelled among the dead on the floors of his palace. He made love to the moon. A provincial governor, Lucius Vitellus, encountered Caligula during one of his conversations with the divine planet. Caligula asked him if he, too, had seen the goddess. The man saved his life by replying that "Only you gods, Master, can see one another". He was enraged at the refusal of the Jews to worship him, and ordered his image to be placed in the Temple at Jerusalem. This almost plunged Rome into a provincial war, and he reluctantly backed down.

The god dined in splendour with his favourite horse, Incitatus, serving loaves of gold bread to his guests. Incitatus, who had a marble stall and ivory manger, was his most trusted adviser. Caligula recognized the value of his loyalty, and announced that he intended to make the horse a Consul of the Roman people, as a preparatory step to full Senatorial rank and eventual rule over the Empire. He would see how the horse shaped up to the job.

The eventual assassins were Senators, Tribunes and Prefects from the Imperial guard; all close associates of Caligula. One

53

Dictators

Tribune, Cassius Charea, had a particular grudge against Caligula. Cassius had to obtain the new password from Caligula every day, and Caligula had taken to choosing sexually explicit ones to mock him. Cassius had become a laughing stock.

The 24 January AD 41 was the last day of the Palatine Games. The night before, Caligula announced he had a dream in which Zeus had kicked him out of Heaven. Some of the conspirators accompanied Caligula to the Games. He got bored, and left after lunch. They cornered him in a narrow, unguarded passage between the Theatre and the Palace. Charea struck the first few blows, putting Caligula on the ground. In the ensuing frenzy, he was stabbed over thirty times.

Chapter Three

Idi Amin:
Monster from the Ashes

Years into his disastrous reign, standing knee-deep in blood and with his country in ruins around him, Idi Amin proudly announced: "Uganda is a paradise in Africa. If you have a shirt and trousers you can live in Uganda for years."

Clearly, he was mad. He was speaking of a state in which enforced self-cannibalism was being used as a means of execution. In fact, his doctor John Kibukamusakie revealed before his sudden and violent death that Amin had actually been receiving treatment for a cocktail of hypomania, bringing on rapid and wildly conflicting ideas, syphilis whose sufferers often experience grand paranoia; and schizophrenia with a dash of general paralysis of the insane thrown in. Otherwise, Idi was on fine form and had recently vowed to erect statues of his two idols, Queen Victoria and Adolf Hitler, and was pursuing his plans to recruit a bodyguard of six-foot-tall, bagpipe-playing Scots. The West didn't know whether to laugh or cry when Idi Amin spoke. In the end he seemed too much of a fool to be taken seriously, but while the world laughed at his latest ludicrous pronouncement – how he had offered to send a cargo of vegetables to Britain to solve their recession or had refused to attend the Commonwealth Games unless the Queen sent a personal aircraft to fetch him complete with Scottish soldiers and a new pair of his size 13 shoes – Amin was probably indulging one of his favourite vices; crushing the genitals of selected victims with his bare hands. No doubt he was laughing too; he was famous for his sense of humour. The sound of his enormous, body-shaking mirth was the last sound thousands

heard through their dying agony, and it was a noise that
haunted Britain as well as Africa, the noise of a monster risen
from the ashes of their Empire.

Amin's words about Uganda had an uncanny echo in them. It
was the young Winston Churchill who had described Uganda as
a "fairy-tale". "You climb up a ladder," he said, "and at the top
there is a wonderful new world."

It did seem that way. Uganda was the pearl of Africa, the
cradle of the Nile, containing the legendary mountains of the
moon which rise 17,000 feet to Equatorial snowfields. The
country is rich and fertile with forest, rolling plain and gentle
hills. The British who arrived there late in the last century found
an ancient, intelligent and cruel civilization among whom
roasting and burial alive were still popular as punishments. It
was also a country riven with historic tribal disputes and enmity
which remain a powerful force even today. There are over forty
tribes with local and family loyalties that make them far more
sympathetic to their own leaders than any overall government.
The ruling monarch was the cruel and despotic Kabuka Butesa
I, king of the dominant Buganda tribe who, in a pronouncement
which Amin would have been proud of, demanded a daughter
of English royalty in return for allowing the Christian missionaries freedom to preach. But in general the British experience in
Uganda was a happy one. However, when the "Wind Of
Change" swept through Africa after World War II and they
withdrew, they left a country which was ill-prepared for
democracy. Although the hastily arranged elections in 1962
brought a Socialist Government led by Milton Obote to power,
there were already allegations of corruption and worse hanging
over ministers, and the tribal disputes were as violent as ever. In
the uncertainty, men who had acquired great authority as loyal
servants of their British rulers benefited from their head-start
and tightened their grip on the reins of power. The future Army
Chief of Staff, Idi Amin, was one of these. In the words of one
contemporary: "He was just the type that the British liked, the
type of African that they used to refer to as from the 'warrior

Idi Amin. *Hulton-Deutsch*

tribes': black, big, uncouth, uneducated and willing to obey orders."

Amin's willingness to obey orders had brought him a long way. He was born in the north of Uganda, the furthest province bordering on the wastes of the Sudan, into one of the smallest tribes, the Kakwa, on 1 May 1928. His mother left her husband and fled south from the tiny mud and wattle village. She supported herself and her growing child by supplying love potions and charms, and Amin's childhood was steeped in superstition and old tribal legends. A decidedly large boy, he became a natural leader among the village children, having discovered, even at this early age, how sensitive the testicles of his playfellows were.

In 1946 he enlisted in the King's African Rifles. He had developed quite serious military ambitions, and was very attracted by the mystique and traditions of the British army but it took him seven years of hard graft to make lance-corporal even in a regiment where intelligence was not necessarily considered a virtue. Obedience and enthusiasm were preferable, and there he had his admirers. "Not much grey matter, but a splendid chap to have about," said one British officer. People liked him; he made them laugh. The Europeans thought the world of him. He showed pride in his regiment, his boots were always spotless and he excelled on the sports field. Six foot four inches tall and weighing in at his peak at twenty stone, he became heavyweight boxing champion of Uganda. Slowly he inched up the ranks as the British, faced with the problem of which Africans to make officers opted for those who, however illiterate, were at least strong and loyal. Amin was semi-literate, and could speak a little English. In spite of failing to complete military training courses in both England and Israel he was, by 1960, a lieutenant.

There is a story originating from this time which shows how simple he still was. His commanding officer, Major Graham, persuaded Amin to open a bank account. He duly deposited £10, but within a few hours had spent £2000. Swaggering through town in his uniform he had purchased new suits, a car and an indecent amount of food and drink. It was the grand behaviour of a king, a role he obviously relished. There were other stories as well, not so humorous. Rumours of atrocities committed in distant frontier villages by soldiers of the King's African Rifles, of captives trussed up and bayoneted and common to these rumours was the figure of a big, happy, laughing officer with a particular line in sadism. Someone should have seen, but it was the eve of independence and the British had other things on their minds, and besides, Lieutenant Amin seemed to get the job done.

After independence, with the British officers gone, Amin's career took off. True, some mud did stick to him, but it was curiously difficult to find anyone living to back up the allegations of cruelty and illegal gold, ivory and coffee smuggling. He was Deputy Commander of the Army when in 1966, the Prime Minister, Milton Obote, asked him for help.

Obote had tried to resolve the conflict between tribal loyalties and the legal government by appointing the traditional King, still from the large Buganda tribe to the position of President to assure the Buganda that they still exercised authority within a government which was dominated by members of other, smaller tribes. Obote himself was from the minority Langi tribe. Thus the improbably named Edward William Walugembe Luwangula Mutesa III, thirty-fifth Kabuka of Buganda, otherwise known as "King Freddie", assumed what was intended to be a largely ceremonial position. A rift rapidly developed, and when Obote tried to reduce Freddie's powers, the Buganda tribe rebelled.

Amin responded in typical style to Obote's request that he flex some muscle. He assaulted the Presidential Palace with a 122mm gun mounted on his own jeep, knocking great chunks out of the walls. In fighting, 1,500 Buganda died, and King Freddie fled to Britain where he died. Obote came to rely on Amin and his forthright approach to problems.

They say "he who sups with the devil must use a long spoon".

Dictators

Obote supped with Amin until 1971. Growing discontent with the Government's increasing bureaucracy and corruption formed a backdrop to this unfortunate marriage, and in 1969 there was an assassination attempt on Obote. It failed and Obote survived, unlike one Brigadier Okoya who was foolish enough to doubt Amin's loyalty during the crisis. Both he and his wife mysteriously died. The relationship between Amin and Obote cooled. Obote had good cause to fear Amin, who in turn suspected he was being squeezed out and the air was thick with rumours of Amin's impending arrest when in January 1971, Obote flew off to Singapore to attend the Commonwealth Conference. It was to prove one of the longest business trips in history; he would not be able to return for nine years. In his absence, Uganda fell victim to a man whose staggering incompetence ran a close second to his genuine pleasure in murder. Nothing that is said about Idi Amin can be worse than the truth.

The coup Amin launched on 25 January 1971 was a traditional affair. Starting at 3 a.m., the army stormed the Parliament, the airport (killing two priests) and the radio station. Telephones and telex lines were cut. Amin watched the proceedings from his luxurious and now heavily fortified mansion situated in Prince Charles Drive on one of Kampala's seven imposing hills. It became known as The Command Post. Surrounded by tanks, it bristled with barbed wire and machine-guns.

In the aftermath of the coup, there was a strange, carnival atmosphere. The anti-Obote crowds took to the streets, breaking the curfew and hailing Major-General Amin as their saviour. They were principally Buganda tribesmen who resented Obote's expulsion of their King. Amin denounced Obote as a corrupt Communist. He would ensure free elections and then return his troops to barracks, he declared to the outside world as he took to the streets and countryside, stopping looting and dispensing personal cheques to the population, which naturally earned their approval. He also freed some political prisoners and allowed the Buganda to bring the body of the dead King Freddie back for burial. One British observer wrote: "I have never encountered a more benevolent and apparently popular leader than General Amin."

But if Idi Amin was going to prepare the country for elections, he was doing so in a strange way. Within three weeks of his coup, 2,000 army officers and men died on his orders; within three months, 10,000 civilians were slaughtered. Perhaps he thought the electoral roll needed shortening.

The murder began in a systematic and initially secretive way. The prime targets were members of the Acholi and Langi tribes – the tribes of Milton Obote and other potential rivals. Obote's brother-in-law and his family were wiped out. Killer squads fostered by Amin within the army were unleashed. When in doubt of their next victims, they simply chose names beginning with "O", as this was a common characteristic of Acholi and Langi names. The soldiers had absolute powers of arrest; the names of these new organizations were both chillingly ambiguous and hideously inappropriate: "The Public Safety Unit"; "The State Research Bureau".

Thirty-six senior officers from the unlucky tribes were summoned to Mackindye prison for "training in internal security". They were locked in cells and bayoneted at leisure.

The former Army Chief of Staff, Brigadier Hussein Suleiman, whose appointment Amin had once deeply resented was arrested and beaten slowly to death with rifle butts and wrenches. According to some, his head subsequently disappeared, only to reappear deep frozen, in the hands of a marauding Amin at an infamous dinner party a year later. Suleiman's was possibly the first head in a collection that became so extensive it required its own refrigerator.

At Mbarara and Jinja barracks the officer corps were crushed by tanks as they mustered on the parade grounds to salute Amin. Elsewhere, others were apparently herded into rooms and grenades lobbed through the windows. In the prisons and cells of Mackindye, Naguru and Nakasero limbs were smashed with sledgehammers and car-axles, and prisoners were compelled to kill each other with 16lb sledgehammers in the vain hope that they would be spared. Then the hammers were given to others to whom the same promise was made, and the chain killings went on until the overflowing human jam of eyes, teeth and bone tissue was shovelled onto trucks like garden refuse and dumped in the rivers, lakes and forests outside Kampala. When the lights went out in Kampala, the story goes, the locals knew that forty miles away at the Owen Falls Dam on Lake Victoria, the hydro-electric generators were once again clogged with bodies.

Whilst Amin pursued his genocidal course, his government was officially recognized by Britain amongst others, and Idi launched himself upon the international scene with all the charming naivety of a debutante. He was finally playing the Imperial role he fancied for himself. Dressed in full military attire with a museum's worth of medals pinned to his chest, he visited Israel and England. Israel took Amin seriously. Here was a friendly Moslem leader of an African country; through Uganda, Israel could have access to the strategically important Sudan. The Israelis were a bit perturbed by their conversations with Amin, one of which went something like this:

"I would like twenty-four Phantom Jets."

"Why?"

"I need to bomb Tanzania."

It was that much-admired straightforwardness again; Amin's ambitions were obviously not limited to his own country. When the military hardware he demanded from Israel was not forthcoming his attitude changed. In 1972, after Palestinian terrorists murdered Israeli athletes at the Olympic Games in Munich he sent an extraordinary telegram to Kurt Waldheim, the United Nations Secretary General, and Golda Meir, the Israeli Prime Minister, in which he informed them:

"Germany is the right place, where, when Hitler was Prime Minister and Supreme Commander, he burnt over six million Jews. This is because Hitler and all the German people know that the Israelis are not people who are working in the interest of the people of the world and that is why they burned the Israelis alive with gas in the soil of Germany . . ."

This was just one of the many shocking and incoherent messages he was liable to dash off to world leaders when the mood took him, sometimes giving advice on their political and personal problems, at others simply taunting them. The Prime Minister and the Queen of Britain were favourite targets. Whilst Amin adored and aped the style of the colonial Empire, he took a special delight in tormenting England. On his inauguration as President he had his huge body carried aloft by Europeans to symbolize "the white man's burden", and announced that he was "the Conqueror of the British Empire".

The highlights of his first official visit to Britain, where he was preferred to the left-wing Obote, included dinners and parties with Conservative Prime Minister Edward Heath and the Queen and Prince Philip. He also went to Scotland, where he acquired his fetish for things Scottish and where the official reception obviously went to his head; a few years later he decided that the Scots wanted him as King, an honour he would be happy to accept. Amin also made a familiar request for arms and Harrier Jets on the pretext that he simply had to bomb South Africa, Tanzania, and Sudan. The British began, too late, to realize what a monster they had helped give birth to.

Back at home the process of good government was made difficult by a shortage of living Cabinet Ministers. Uganda was not an impoverished country, but the incompetence of Amin soon began to triumph. He had no economic policies, apart from extortion, and his speech at the inaugural meeting of the so-called Uganda Development Bank showed his unorthodox approach to finance: "Every one hundred years, God appoints one person to be very powerful in the world to follow what the Prophet directed. When I dream, then things are put into practice . . ."

The dreams were another problem; Amin was in touch with God and Uganda was now being ruled by his visions. "The problem takes on fantastic dimensions," said one Minister. "He cannot concentrate . . . he does not read . . . he cannot write. He has to have recourse to people of his own intelligence and calibre – the illiterate army officers who rule the country . . ."

Dictators

Most of the army officers were now former drivers and cooks who had become majors and colonels. Military spending went up five hundred per cent. Inflation soared to seven hundred per cent; a bar of soap cost two weeks' wages. Amin's solution was to print more money, whilst annexing the foreign reserves for his own use. Special flights to London and Paris took Amin's cronies, their pockets stuffed with Uganda's dwindling cash, on spending sprees for luxury goods. The killing of politicians and civilians continued at a breathtaking pace. The Church was another target. The Archbishop of Uganda died in a "motor accident" along with two Government Ministers, and Amin personally shot Archbishop Luwun, telling his aides that he had "lost his temper". The killer squads had complete control of the country. When not eliminating suspected opponents they were simply killing people for their possessions; they had to be paid somehow. One ingenious method was to take people off the streets, murder them and then charge their relatives for the recovery of their mutilated corpses. So much to do, so little time; it was hardly surprising they fell behind with the work. In one incident a former civil servant, Frank Kalimazo, was attending a wedding when he heard that his "disappearance" had been announced over the radio. He was part of the backlog.

News of this hell-on-earth did reach the outside world, but so staggering was it that it was only slowly believed. It was difficult to confirm. Two young American journalists, Nicholas Stroh and Robert Siedle, who, early in the regime had begun to ask questions about the army massacres, were gunned down at Mbarara barracks. Their murderer, Major Juma Aigu, a former taxi driver, reputedly drove about Kampala in Stroh's Volkswagen. Refugees and exiles began to tell terrible stories. Education Minister Edward Rugomayo escaped and detailed a lengthy list of atrocities including slow deaths by bleeding and amputation, genital mutilation, people being fed on their own flesh until they died, reproductive organs being set on fire, electric shocks and the gouging out of eyes. Some of the equipment being used for this was imported from Britain by Amin's close adviser, the "Mephistopheles of Uganda", English exile Bob Astles, Head of the "Anti-Corruption Unit". Astles suffered the fate he had condemned so many to. His decomposing body turned up in the grounds of a hotel after Amin's eventual fall. It was dangerous to take gifts from Amin. Bob McKenzie, another white ally and former Kenyan Minister who quarrelled with Amin, flew out of Kampala clutching a kiss-and-make-up gift from him, a lion's head trophy. It exploded mid-air.

Amin's home life was no less remarkable. He had a harem of wives and twenty-five to thirty-five children. It is alleged that when Kay, one of his wives (whom he had recently divorced) died in a botched abortion attempt, he ordered the surgeons to cut her up and reassemble her with her legs on her shoulders and arms on her pelvis as a warning to the others. On the testimony of his housekeeper it is known that he kept the head of Jesse Gitta, the former husband of his wife Sarah, in the fridge in his "Botanical Room". She discovered it after her marriage, along with the head of Ruth Kobusinje, a girl he was sleeping with and suspected of infidelity. One nurse describes decapitating six bodies and sending the shaved, preserved heads to Amin. Nobody knows what he wanted them for, which is odd, as he usually left nothing to the imagination. Henry Kyemba, the Ugandan health minister, confessed from the safety of foreign exile: "I am ashamed to admit that on several occasions he told me quite proudly that he had eaten the organs or flesh of his human victims."

Back overseas Amin switched his loyalty from Israel to Libya, supporting the anti-Jewish and anti-Western policies of the eccentric Gaddafi in return for military support and cash most of which he stashed away for his own use, buying three villas outside Libya's capital, Tripoli. Gaddafi was under the mistaken impression that Uganda was a Moslem country, Amin assured him that eighty per cent of the population were followers of Islam; it was actually nearer fifteen per cent. To please Libya he expelled the Israeli engineers who built his Entebbe airport and who were working on vital dam projects. He now saw himself as

Dictators

the champion of the Third World against the Imperial West. In spite of his risible offers to Britain and America to sort out Northern Ireland and Vietnam for them in his own brutal way, he styled himself the opponent of colonialism, which won him support among Africans even as he murdered them, so eager were they for a champion against the West; at least, they thought, he has their attention. "I consider myself the most powerful figure in the world," he said. "I am the greatest politician in the world. I have shaken the British so much I deserve a degree in philosophy." He confiscated British property, but simultaneously started the "Save Britain Fund", to "help Britain through its economic crisis". He fired off another telegram to Edward Heath saying that Britain's state was a disgrace to the rest of the Commonwealth, but offering to organize a whipround amongst Uganda's friends, "If you will let me know the exact position of the mess." How they must have hated those patronizing telegrams.

Amin's neighbours in Tanzania and the Sudan were not spared his sabre-rattling. He made claims on their territory, and it was only with great effort that Tanzania could restrain itself. As usual, Idi would threaten one moment and the next he would fire off a conciliatory telegram. "I love you very much," he wrote to President Julius Nyerere. "And if you were a woman I would consider marrying you." It was Nyerere who was to eventually bring Amin down.

There were two remarkable events which put this grinning Satan in the centre of the international limelight. The first was the expulsion of the Asians, and the second was the Entebbe hijack.

In a move which dealt a death-blow to the economy, Amin expelled the entire Asian population of Uganda, who ran about eighty per cent of the country's small businesses. "Asians came to Uganda to build the railway. The railway is finished. They must leave now," he pronounced, having once again been counselled by the voice of God. The Asians were told they could take their possessions but were habitually stripped of everything, even their bedding and watches. Most of the Asians had to seek asylum in Britain. When Amin thought that the British High Commission were not processing the Asians fast enough, he kidnapped one hundred British citizens and held them until the Commission worked a twelve-hour day and hired more premises and staff. The businesses were handed over to his tribal henchmen. The shelves were soon empty, the shops closed; Uganda became a desert; people were near starvation, but Amin, still dwelling in his fantasy world, offered help simultaneously to thirty-two Third World countries afflicted by drought. As far as he was concerned, he could still write cheques, so there was no problem.

The Entebbe affair began with the hijacking of an Air France airliner carrying three hundred passengers from Tel Aviv to Paris by Palestinian terrorists. Amin had allied himself with the Palestinian Liberation Organization as part of his anti-Jewish, anti-Western bravado, and the airliner was allowed to land at Entebbe airport, from where the hijackers issued a string of demands. The passengers were to die in forty-eight hours unless fifty-three terrorists imprisoned in Israel and Europe were released. The eyes and cameras of the world were turned on Uganda. Amin revelled in it; he was instrumental in holding the West to ransom. An extension of the deadline was negotiated and the non-Jewish passengers released. The hostages were taken to the airport terminal. Amin passed among them, smiling benevolently. One old lady, Dora Bloch, a joint British and Israeli citizen, choked on her food, and had to be taken to Kampala's hospital. She missed her chance to live, as while she was away, Israeli commandos staged a spectacular rescue. Landing at the airport, they routed Amin's soldiers and destroyed a flight of Mig fighters that were lined up. One hour and sixteen minutes later they flew out of Entebbe leaving all seven kidnappers and twenty Ugandan troops dead and taking with them all the hostages. All, that is, except Dora Bloch.

When Amin heard, he was paralysed with fury. His hour of glory had turned into deep humiliation. The first victim of his anger was the little old lady, Dora Bloch. She was taken from the hospital and shot. Her body was dumped on wasteland on the outskirts of Kampala. It was made a capital offence to talk about the affair. Two Kampala girls vanished after joking that their boyfriends were "strong as Israeli Pilots". Amin sent Israel yet another insane telegram threatening to attack them unless compensation was paid for his destroyed aircraft – he was particularly upset about these – as well as "expenses" he had incurred "entertaining" the hostages.

It had to end. People find it astonishing that he lasted so long, but the West was reluctant to intervene in a country that had only recently gained its independence; besides, for the British, he was an embarrassment, and they preferred to try and ignore him in the hope that, like the bogeyman of nightmares, he would just disappear. If they intervened, they would be accused of colonialism and risked turning Amin into a hero. They couldn't win, and he rubbed their noses in it. The other African states were reluctant to become publicly involved in possibly bloody fighting amongst themselves; they too hoped he would vanish. Libya still actively supported him. Within his country, Amin was protected by the tribal henchmen he had elevated and whose lifestyles were dependent on him. He was surrounded by military hardware. He carried a loaded, cocked gun at all times. It was advisable not to make any sudden movements in his presence. That was how he survived; by exploiting the fears of others. He may have been incoherent, clinically mad, illiterate and savage, but he had an animal cunning which told him which parts of a person, in mind as well as body, hurt when he squeezed them. Moreover, there was nothing complicated about his needs, which made them all the easier to supply and protect; he got the same pleasure from murder as from eating and often combined the two for convenience and satisfaction.

In Idi Amin, primitive tribal brutality was mixed with a fixation for the military trappings of Empire to hideously comic effect. The bully-boy qualities that made him so useful to the British rulers of Uganda as a servant came to horrible fruition when he became the master; in serving their interests they had put the means to power in the hands of a man who was an unmitigated disaster for the whole continent of Africa. It was a tragic legacy; it was one of history's worst jokes.

In October 1978, Amin carried out one of his long-standing threats and sent 3,000 troops into Tanzania. They raped and massacred their way through the countryside. Amin announced he had conquered Tanzania. When President Julius Nyerere retaliated and Amin's troops were driven back, Amin frantically suggested that he and Nyerere settle the war with a boxing match refereed by Mohammed Ali. The Tanzanians continued to advance and by the Spring of 1979 they were on the outskirts of Kampala. In vain Amin called for a last stand at Jinja; the troops didn't show up and neither did Amin; he had already fled to hide behind the skirts of his ally, Colonel Gaddafi in Libya. He spent the next few years there until even Gaddafi could take no more and kicked him out. There were rumours of some unpleasant business involving Amin and Gadafi's fourteen-year-old daughter. He and his family finally found a haven from extradition in Saudi Arabia, where he lived in luxurious comfort, on stolen Ugandan money, until his death in August 2003.

In Uganda, when Tanzanian troops entered the office of the Head of the State Research Bureau, they found a framed epigram. It read:

"No wisdom is greater than kindness. Those who build their success on others' misfortunes are never successful."

It was unlikely that the previous occupant had been able to read. In any case, it was a most inappropriate moral all round.

Chapter Four

Genghis Khan: Sacker of Cities

There can be no greater testament to the enduring terror of Genghis Khan than the title he is still known by among the Muslim writers of Persian nations whose cultured Empire he destroyed seven centuries ago. They call him "The Accursed". Many of the great cities he razed in China, the Middle East and the Caucasus have never recovered their former status; some have never been rebuilt, and their ruins still retain an eerie, desolate silence. It is the kind of oppressive atmosphere that hangs over places where, at one time, all living creatures have been systematically slaughtered.

It was not that he took any pleasure in the business. The Mongols were strictly pragmatic about the slaughter. As they advanced, they simultaneously wished to secure themselves against any uprising behind them. Their army was always outnumbered by the population, so they were simply re-adjusting the odds. There was an obvious psychological spin-off from this, in that the terror the news of these tactics inflicted on the next city understandably reduced the will of the defenders. Frequently they offered to surrender, so long as the population might be spared. Often, the Mongols would agree, and then kill them anyway. They did not regard this as treachery, just good military sense; they shouldn't look a gift-horse in the mouth.

After they took a city, either by siege or subterfuge, there was a fairly standard menu of behaviour. First, they plundered in a very democratic fashion and drove the population outside the city walls, where they would be assembled and men and women divided. Of the men, those with useful skills might be enslaved

Ghengis Khan. *Hulton-Deutsch*

and returned to Mongolia. Other young men would be taken for military purposes. The Mongols used these as unarmed cannon-fodder in their assaults, herding several thousand in front of them as they swept down on their enemy, as if stampeding cattle. The remainder would be killed, generally decapitated, and their heads stacked in neat pyramids. The women were, without exception, raped. A few might be taken for slaves or concubines, and the rest also killed. If an example was to be made of a particular city, then no-one would be spared, for any purpose. The inhabitants might be driven out through a gate and decapitated as they walked through it, in a sort of ghastly conveyor belt. Sometimes each Mongol soldier was designated a number of executions to perform, which on occasion was as high as five hundred per man. This could take days to perform, even with the famous stamina of the Mongol troops, particularly if the order was given that no living thing was to escape. Even dogs and cats were then executed and babies in the womb were run through with swords. This was all performed in a highly disciplined fashion. Finally the city would be set on fire and afterwards flooded where conditions permitted. The prospect of all this happening produced some fairly drastic reactions. At Peking, 60,000 women threw themselves off the city walls rather than face tea with the Mongols; when the siege left them starving, the whole population resorted to cannibalism rather than surrender.

The advance of the Mongol hordes is one of the most signifi-cant historical events of the last thousand years. Quite apart from the destruction they wrought, they completely altered the distribution of people, wealth and disease within the known world. But the home life of Genghis Khan, whose name is legendary, is something of a mystery.

He was born plain Temuchin on the banks of the Onon river in 1162. Mongolia, his homeland, is the vast, high plateau between the forests of Siberia in the north and the wastes of the Gobi desert in the south. At the time of his birth, the Mongols were a collection of nomadic tribes, with occasional, but unreliable alliances. Among them, his father was leader of a sizable group of clans. They lived on the move, in tents, and had no conception of organized town life. In fact, they could see no virtue in society as understood by others, which partly explains their lack of remorse in destroying all those they overran. Temuchin's father, a chieftain of the Borjigid clan named Yesukai, died when he was aged nine. He had been returning from arranging the betrothal of his young son to Borte, an equally young wife, when he was poisoned by some Tartars.

It was a Mongol tradition that a new-born be named after the most important event that occurred immediately before the birth, and hence Temuchin was appropriately named after a chieftain that Yesukai had killed shortly before his son's arrival.

In his new-born baby's hand Yesukai had observed a stone the colour of coagulated blood, a powerful omen of the infant's potential greatness. The Mongols were a superstitious race. They had no organized, public religion, but believed all sorts of shamanism, oracles, magic and images. There was also one overall god, Tengri. The Mongols regarded the tops of mountains and the origins of springs as sacred to these higher powers, and even revered the spirit of water. It was considered sacrilege to wash clothes, cooking utensils or bodies in water, with devastating consequences to personal hygiene, which did not exist. They were a ripe, smelly bunch, capable of enduring the most unimaginable hardships in temperatures as low as –42, where the encrusted dirt helped to provide protection against the deadly cold. In their own myths, they were the offspring of a blue wolf.

The early life of Temuchin was spent in struggle and poverty. His father's death had broken up the clan alliance, with many tribes refusing to swear allegiance to the boy. According to Mongol legend, he began his rise to power with only two arrows to his name. His mother, Ho'elun, a tough and canny woman, succeeded in holding some allies together, and he also received protection from a former blood-brother of his father. His mother's counsel saved his life on a number of occasions. The

Dictators

Mongols were polygamous but women were also regarded as wise companions, who wielded considerable influence through their advice which was frequently sought. For thirty years he waged an unceasing war against the neighbouring tribes and the former allies of his father, until in 1206, he felt strong enough to call himself Ruler of an Empire, a title which was confirmed by his official election by representatives of the now subdued and loyal followers. The many strongholds, hiding places and battle-grounds of these early years became sacred places to the Mongols, who conferred on him the name Genghis Khan, meaning "Perfect Warrior".

After all these years of warring, Genghis Khan had amassed considerable military expertise, and, as early explorers noted, there was a remarkable discipline among his troops. Discipline was a feature of the Mongol world that evolved under him. Although frequent drunkenness on the obligatory fermented mare's milk was a traditional and substantial part of life, there was little serious quarrelling or crime among the Mongols themselves, and they reserved murder for their enemies. Loyalty was much valued, with oaths sealed by the drinking of blood, and the ceremonial slaughter of horses. The vast and impeccably co-ordinated military operations that Genghis Khan now under-took depended upon skills that were perfected in the huge hunting expeditions the clans would make. The Mongols were principally meat-eaters, and happy to chew on anything with a decent calorific value, be it rabbit, rat or wolf. They had a particular penchant for horse, but as all their army was cavalry and their way of life depended on their tough, stocky horses, they only ate them in dire circumstances. The meat from these was so tough, they would stick it under a saddle and ride it until it was tender, marinating it between their thighs.

These huge hunts could take one to three months. The entire Mongol army might be deployed on them. This army, at its greatest strength and including the various auxiliaries, slaves and reserves, was probably never greater than 120,000. The entire population of the region was unlikely to have been more than 500,000. On a great hunt, the army would cordon off an area occupying thousands of miles, and slowly but thoroughly begin to herd every living creature, over hill and through forest, towards a central killing ground no bigger than nine miles. As described by witnesses, the scene was mind-boggling. Lions, wolves, bears, deer, yak, asses and hares were driven together in their hundreds of thousands, killing, mating, panicking, eating and sleeping. An apocalyptic picture, accompanied by the discordant, awful shriek of the frightened animals. No killing whatsoever was allowed until Genghis Khan arrived at the scene with his entourage and wives and took up a good position from which to overlook the entertainment. After he gave permission for the hunting to begin, the chase, slaughter and feeding would go on for days.

The first object of this new military power was the Jurchen Dynasty of China, who considered themselves the masters of the Mongolian Steppes. From 1206–1211, Genghis Khan punched a hole through the neighbouring Tangut territory towards China, about which he accumulated as much military intelligence as possible. He only had one enemy on the Mongolian Steppes to worry about, Kushlek the Naiman Khan, who had fled after a sizable defeat to the Irtysh river, where Genghis routed him again, and from there to the Khitian Tartars, seeking support from neighbouring Persia. Kushlek would remain a thorn in his side. The operation against China was highly successful, with a string of victories encouraging desertion to the Mongolians and the terror that went in advance of them persuading garrisons to surrender without a fight. The army, split into three prongs, moved with phenomenal speed. By 1214, Genghis Khan was able to say to the Jurchen Emperor: "By the decree of heaven you are now as weak as I am strong, but I am willing to retire from my conquests . . . as a condition of my doing so it will be necessary for you to distribute largesse to my officers and men to appease their fierce hostility."

Appease them he did, with 3,000 horses, two royal princesses, five hundred young men and girls, a herd of white camels and as much swag as they could carry. Genghis Khan went back to Mongolia, leaving an army to mop up. However, the Jurchen were not completely subdued, and the war against the Chinese would go on after his death.

Back in Mongolia, Genghis Khan came up against his old friend, Kushlek. He had ingratiated himself with his hosts, the Khitian Tartars and then, with consummate treachery, enlisted the help of the Persian neighbours to usurp the existing ruler, who was forced to abdicate in favour of his former guest. Kushlek then measured up to Genghis Khan once more, who again defeated him, and this time managed to put him to death. As Kushlek counted as nobility, and it was forbidden to shed the blood of nobles, Genghis had him suffocated under a pile of carpets. The Mongols had a number of ingenious ways to circumvent this regulation, and at other times nobles were strangled with a bow-string, or buried alive.

Kushlek's ill-gotten kingdom now became part of the Mongol Empire. A curious consequence of this was that, for a brief time, Genghis Khan became something of an Islamic hero. Kushlek had treated the Moslems of his hijacked realm badly, but Genghis Khan and his Mongol hordes were tolerant in matters of religion, and when the dial was not set to "massacre", the Mongols could be very easygoing generally, preferring parties to pogroms. His position as saviour of the Moslem world did not last long.

His territories now extended up to the border with the Khwarizm Empire of Eastern Iran/Iraq. Genghis was eager to establish trade links with other nations; trade was also another means of diplomatic dialogue. After he had encountered merchants from the Khwarizm Empire, he sent a Mongol delegation back to the Khwarizm ruler, Shah Mohammed, with a message of intended peace couched in evocative terms:

"We have . . . dispatched to your country a group of merchants in order that they may acquire the wondrous wares of those regions; and that henceforth the abscess of evil thoughts may be lanced by the improvement of relations and agreement between us and the pus of sedition and rebellion removed . . ."

If the delegation bearing this message had reached Mohammed, who was keen on peace and trade, the Mongol advance might have stopped right there, instead of coming to the very doors of Europe, and several million people would probably have lived. Unfortunately, then followed one of the more significant mistakes in history.

At the border town of Otrar, the governor was a rather stupid, suspicious and greedy man named Inaljuk. He was ignorant of any proposed dialogue between Mohammed and the Mongols, and didn't bother to check the official position with Mohammed before massacring the delegation on the grounds that they were spies and seizing their goods.

Genghis Khan demanded satisfaction, which Mohammed was too proud to concede, sending the Mongol envoys back minus their beards. What began as a punitive expedition by the Mongols soon turned into a Blitzkrieg invasion which took them through Khwarizm into Armenia and Russia, capturing almost the entire Middle East.

The Mongols attacked with four armies under the command of Genghis Khan's various sons and himself. Mohammed faced them with an army of 400,000, and quickly lost 160,000 of these in a spectacular rout. The Mongols' capacity to co-ordinate vast, tactical troop movements on several simultaneous fronts and proceed according to minutely devised plans was simply too sophisticated for the Moslem forces, who favoured the open, pitched battle. In addition, the Mongols had picked up a whole new range of siege machinery in their Chinese wars, and now put these to good use as city after city fell to them. Otrar fell, then Khojent, Tashkent and Nur. Bokhara, "The City of Science", was utterly destroyed, and Merv, one of the legendary jewels of Moslem civilization and home of the "1001 Nights of Arabia" was burned to the ground. Merv surrendered after making one of those unwise bargains with the Mongols and 700,000 people were killed. These were only some of the cities that were obliterated in the Mongol advance. The populous centre of Herat was spared initially.

Dictators

Mohammed died of pleurisy, much regretting his earlier pride. His son, the gallant Jelaliddin, took up the fruitless battle against Genghis Khan, who pursued him relentlessly, whilst developing a healthy admiration for his courage. In 1221, Jelaliddin raised enough support to start a serious uprising, but after bitter fighting the Persian forces were defeated and Jelaliddin only escaped by jumping twenty foot into a river on his horse, which impressed Genghis considerably. Jelaliddin escaped to Delhi, out of the Mongols' reach, and Genghis had to console himself with ravaging the Asian provinces of Peshawar and Lahore.

In the meantime, one or two cities which had initially co-operated to avoid destruction, rebelled. Herat was one of these, and it is here that 1,600,000 are recorded as having been killed in methodical executions lasting a week. At Nishapur, where one of his favourite commanders was killed, Genghis Khan decreed: "That the town be laid waste, that the site be ploughed upon and that in the exaction of vengeance not even cats and dogs should be left alive . . ."

By 1222, the Mongols, conquerors of China and the Middle East, had advanced through Astrakhan to the Don river, where the Russians stood, dismayed at this strange, invincible enemy.

The mobility, toughness and discipline of the Mongol army was a new phenomenon. The Mongols were stocky troops, and their army was exclusively cavalry. Each man had at least one spare mount, often three or four of the squat strong horses that roamed the Mongolian steppes. The soldier wore a fur cap with protective ear pieces for casual wear, and a leather and metal helmet for combat. On his horse he carried a vast array of tools and weapons; two bows, and several quivers of arrows, a lance with a hook on it for pulling people off horses, an axe, a lasso, sharpening stone, kettle and a few emergency rations. These consisted of about ten pounds of curdled milk dried in the sun. When required, about half a pound was dissolved with enough water to make a foul-smelling, cheesy syrup. The men literally lived on their horses, and could happily sleep in the saddle. The horse also enabled them to cross seemingly impassable rivers, as they would float across on a bundle of possessions, holding on to the tail of their mount. The Mongol cavalryman could go for several days without a cooked meal, and if necessary would open up a vein in the neck of his horse and suck some of the blood, afterwards closing up the wound. His proficiency with bow and arrow was such that he could hit a man at 200–400 metres.

The psychology of inducing terror was an important part of the Mongolian war-plan. In this, the massacres, and rumours of massacres played their part. Although their army was generally smaller than the opposing forces, they deliberately built up the illusion of a vast "horde". The horses helped with this, and they would often mount dummies on their spare horses to give the impression that their army was three or four times its actual size. At night, each soldier lit several torches; from the walls of a besieged city, these myriad, misleading pin-pricks of flame must have been demoralizing evidence of their army's numbers.

They had another secret weapon; their total lack of hygiene. The Mongol hordes stank to high heaven; their approach could be smelled miles away, as they advanced in terrifying, completely controlled silence. And then, in attack, the stench of the great, unwashed Mongol hordes and their horses was both so potent and alien that defenders became paralysed with nausea and fear.

It was this enemy that the Russians faced. The Mongols sent envoys, and the Russians made the fatal mistake of killing them, thus precipitating a conflict in which the Mongols rampaged throughout Bulgaria, and even penetrated as far north as Novgorod, after which they returned, stuffed with booty, to Mongolia. It seems that the basis of the nation's economy was loot from their expeditions.

Having given the Europeans a taste of things to come in future years, Genghis Khan turned his attention once more to China, and particularly its southern regions which still eluded him. Along with the booty, he had acquired a growing appreciation for the benefits of education from the Chinese, and determined that, illiterate though he was, his sons should be able to read and write. He had splendid sons who all distinguished themselves in the massacres of his military campaigns, but were also noted for wildness and alcoholism even among a nation of serious drinkers. Under Genghis Khan and with the Chinese influence, Mongol society became a closer-knit structure, with a distinct aristocracy, the "Golden Family", and a strict code of laws, the Yasa. Genghis Khan became interested in Chinese mysticism, and heard about a learned Taoist monk, Ch'ang-Ch'un, renowned for his knowledge of Taoist alchemy which pursued the elixir of life. Genghis Khan, mistaking the pursuit of the philosophic idea as indication of the elixir's actual existence, became convinced that this man might know where he could find the philosopher's stone that would confer immortality on him. With this, he intended to subjugate the heavenly powers to his will. He ordered the monk to be fetched. It was a journey of 3,108 miles and well over a year before they actually met. When they did, and Genghis Khan asked the monk where the means to immortality lay, he was forced to reply that "There are many means of prolonging life, but no medicine of immortality". Surprisingly, Genghis Khan, although naturally disappointed, thanked the monk courteously for his honesty, and consulted with him about Taoist philosophy for several days. After the monk's departure, they maintained contact until death came for the Perfect Warrior in 1227.

Campaigning in southern China, he derived from the conjunction of the planets that evil awaited him, and turned homewards. At the Si-Kiang river in Kansuh he fell ill and died. He had named his son Ogatai as his successor, but until he was securely enthroned, news of Genghis Khan's death was savagely suppressed to prevent instability. Any witnesses of the procession of his body back to Mongolia were executed, including many casual travellers. In keeping with Mongolian custom, the location of his tomb was kept secret, and the slaves who carried his body were killed. Horses were stampeded over the place of burial to remove all traces of his interment . . . The Mongolian Emperors have no burial mounds, and no one will ever disturb the resting place of the "Conqueror of the World".

Chapter Five

Nicolae Ceaucescu:
A Family Affair

Rumania is a country where fact and fiction, history and horror-story are freely mixed. The vampires and ghouls of European legend stalk the wilds of Transylvania. Its inhabitants have always been able to describe their present experiences in terms of their mythic past. For many of them, Nicolae Ceaucescu was a reincarnation of that other great Rumanian tyrant, Vlad Dracul, called "The Impaler", popularly thought to be one of the sources for Bram Stoker's *Dracula*.

Nicolae Ceaucescu was born on 26 January 1918 in a two-room peasants cottage in Scornicesti, an unspectacular village a hundred miles or so from Bucharest. He was one of ten children. His mother was a resolute Christian and illiterate, his father a celebrated drunk and bully. The young Nicolae was distinguished by an appalling stutter. An early convert to Communism, it is said that he learned to regurgitate a vast amount of Party dogma by heart to prove his conquest of this impediment. Unfortunately, the stutter remained conspicuous and was secretly much mocked to the end.

The subsequent re-writing of history for propaganda purposes has drawn a risible picture of his early years, full of idealized rosy-cheeked and barefoot peasants, oppressed but cheerfully socialist. Rebuilt, retimbered, whitewashed and spread with suitably working-class straw, his birthplace was opened to the public as a shrine after his ascension to power. There is scarcely a document relating to Ceaucescu's life which has not been altered or simply faked and inserted into the files years afterwards. This mania for tampering with the past extended to the most petty incidents. Photographs of Ceaucescu had to be re-touched to remove any unsightly wrinkles before they were used in publications. The work was dreadfully done, giving the impression that his face had been sand-blasted. In a photograph that appeared in the official newspaper *Scienteia* in 1989, Ceaucescu was seen posing happily with Zhikov the Bulgarian leader, obviously unaware that he had grown a third hand. In the original photograph, Zhikov was holding a hat. It was thought necessary that Ceaucescu should also have a hat, so one was painted in, and a hand added to hold it. The official artist had forgotten to amputate one of the original limbs.

During World War II under the effective rule of the fascist General Ion Atonescu, Rumania actively supported Germany, particularly after the invasion of Russia. Ceaucescu, who had met the future leader of the Rumanian Communist Party, Gheorghiu-Dej, in jail, worked his way up through the junior ranks of the outlawed Party. In 1944 in a coup that was afterwards portrayed as a great Communist uprising, King Michael ousted Ion Antonescu, restored democracy and pulled Rumania out of the war. A coalition government of which the Communists were part, gave them a back door to power. Ceaucescu, recently made Secretary General of the Communist Youth Movement, was off romancing with his bride Elena and took no part in these dramatic proceedings.

Unknown to the Rumanians, their fate was being simultaneously decided at Yalta, where Churchill and Stalin sat down to carve up the wreckage of post-war Europe. With a legendary stroke of the pen, the Russians were given a large chunk of the civilized world, including ninety per cent influence in Rumania, and virtual occupation rapidly followed. Now the Communists became the ruling party.

In the years that followed the fascists were replaced by the Securitate and Russian troops. Opposition was savagely suppressed with liberal use of the cosh and the lie. Democrats were branded as Nazis, condemned by their own confessions extracted under torture. In the General Election of 1946 the

Rumanians overwhelmingly rejected their Communist rulers. Suppressing the results, Gheorghiu-Dej branded the opposition "fascist traitors" and put their leaders on trial. He abolished the popular National Peasants Party and King Michael was forced to abdicate at gunpoint, under the threat that if he didn't go, the Communists would start a civil war. Open season was now declared on the opposition. Between 1945–1955, 280,000 members of the National Peasants Party were arrested, and jailed for a total of 900,000 years. In prison seventy-two per cent of them died of principally unnatural causes.

Ceaucescu did very well out of all this. In 1945, there was a slight set-back when he was fired because he fell out with Moscow's Communist representative, who thought him backward and dim. He bounced back as a dubiously elected deputy to the Rumanian Parliament after the fraudulent 1946 elections and by 1948 he had reached the dizzy heights of Deputy Minister for Agriculture. He took to wearing a badly fitting general's uniform. His passionate nationalism made him popular with the other Rumanian Communists, who were growing increasingly distant from Moscow. In a classically Stalinist piece of career-Communism, he used his promotion to "Secretary to the Central Committee in charge of Party Organization" to ensure that everybody appointed to the endless committees owed their positions to him and knew it. All applications for these positions passed across his desk. He controlled the access to privileges and power in a society where luxuries were desperately sought after. Like Stalin, Ceaucescu's road to power lay in mastering the arts of bureaucracy and graft. He did not move until he felt secure of his support.

The gap between Rumania and Russia continued to widen. There was a strong nationalist streak in the Rumanian Communists and a traditional hatred of Russians among the people. Even after Stalin's death and fall from grace, the Rumanians remained firm believers in his methods. Russia wanted Rumania to be a supplier of grain in the Eastern Bloc's common market. The Rumanian Communists wanted to copy

Dictators

Stalin's industrialization of the Soviet economy. They resented being cast in the role of an agricultural society; they wanted big, stinking factories like the Russians. The upshot was that when Gheorghiu-Dej died in 1965, his body riddled with cancer, the Rumanian Communists looked to quickly elect a leader who would maintain Rumania's relative independence from the Soviet Union; indecision might encourage the Russians to intervene. In this way at the age of forty-seven, Nicolae Ceaucescu, with his strong Stalinist and patriotic views became the Secretary General of the Rumanian Communist Party, and hence the ruler of his country. There were other, better qualified candidates, but they declined to stand against him, knowing that if they opposed and failed they probably wouldn't live. Ceaucescu had arrived at the position of leader without ever having to have an original thought.

Ceaucescu proceeded to implement a frenzy of diplomatic visits and large, heavily staged speeches and public appearances. This ostentatious style became known as "The Frenzy", and it marked the beginnings of his grotesque personality cult. The visits and speeches became increasingly stage-managed and artificial, with motorcades, flower-draped cars, long, dull speeches and balcony appearances in front of orchestrated crowds. He was casting about for a bigger role, both as Communist leader and fervent Rumanian patriot. Something on the world stage, perhaps.

Then he had a huge stroke of luck. In Czechoslovakia, Communism was undergoing a remarkable thaw in the warmth of the "Prague Spring". In 1968 the Russians, who had crushed similar resistance in Hungary, sent the tanks in. This was Ceaucescu's big break. Voicing Rumania's terror of Russian interference he passionately declared:

"There is no justification whatsoever for military intervention in the affairs of a fraternal socialist state . . . the entire Rumanian people will never allow anybody to violate our homeland."

This stirring piece of nationalism miraculously transformed his position. Overnight, the lad from Scornicesti became a national hero and an international sensation.

So delighted were the Western powers to discover an Eastern ally against the Soviet Union, they happily misinterpreted his patriotic rhetoric as progressive thinking worth cultivating. A Communist leader who was anti-Soviet was a prize attraction, and from that moment on they flocked to meet him. De Gaulle, Nixon, and Margaret Thatcher all met the great Nicolae. He could do no wrong. He had become, in Richard Nixon's words, "One of the great leaders of the world". Nixon knew one when he saw one.

It all went to his head. With Western leaders generously manuring his growing personality cult, his ego went spinning dizzily out of control. The "Frenzy" sprouted. Public appearances became completely artificial, with the Securitate leading the applause by the use of tape-recorded clapping. A visit to North Korea, where the demented Kim Il Sung compelled the whole population to wear badges with his face on them, and where every road had a separate lane for his sole use, finally showed Ceaucescu the way forward for Communism.

He was very impressed with the total regimentation of that hideous totalitarian state, as was Elena, who was very concerned her husband should get the respect due to him. After the visit to Korea she became a bossy, demanding career wife, egging the already overbearing Ceaucescu on. Her favourite words to the champion of the Rumanian people were, "They don't deserve you; you are too great for them."

They quickly acquired an entourage of toadies and sycophants only too happy to preserve Ceaucescu from the realities of life in exchange for power and privilege. In common with other similar despots, Ceaucescu rapidly began to believe in his own publicity, the sole content of which was that he was a hero and people loved him.

Lots of things started to disappear and shift mysteriously. It was impossible to trust one's memory or senses. Ceaucescu's old father, drinking as usual in a bar in Bucharest, had told his cronies not to take any notice of his son: "he tells nothing but lies". By daylight, the whole pub had vanished, to be replaced by a long established dairy-outlet. It was not advisable to remark on this. Psychiatric treatment was the favoured punishment for those who saw things differently. At institutions like the Doctor Petra Groza hospital in Bucharest, patients were referred for treatment suffering from odd diseases like "political paranoia". Priests were treated when they complained about corruption; journalists and writers were diagnosed as suffering from "senile dementia" when they wrote about human rights abuses. The political prisoners were locked up with the genuinely disturbed. One case was described as "suffering from": "Persecution complex, neurotic behaviour, delusions, self-preservation drive, discordant character structure; a paranoic, he claims that his flat has been confiscated, and writes numerous complaints . . ."

Finally, when they were genuinely crazed and sick, prisoners were made to build their own coffins and disposed of with drug-

---

The bureaucracy devoted vast efforts to satisfying Ceaucescu's whims. On one occasion he decided that he fancied making a welcome speech to the new students at the polytechnic institute in Bucharest. The only rallying point was currently taken up by a vast, 12,000 cubic metre access hole for the new Bucharest Metro. The morning after his decision, the engineers arriving to work went hay-wire. They had lost their hole. The great, thirty-metre long gash had disappeared. Instead, there were mature trees, grass, flowers; a very pleasant park, perfect for a rally. No-one could bring themselves to tell Ceaucescu that his plans to make the speech were inconvenient, so they were obliged to change reality to conform to his desires. His fantasy now became the only permissible truth.

> General Ion Pacepa describes the drunken Nicu at the height of his powers ordering oysters in a party restaurant, and liberally seasoning them with his own urine before assaulting the waitress over the packed table.

overdoses. Relatives were lucky if they were informed within a year.

Ceaucescu marched triumphantly on. In 1974, he made himself President of Rumania and awarded himself a regal sceptre. The rampant nepotism and family control of Ceaucescu's reign is astonishing. The horrible Elena, who acquired a string of titles to go with her fake degrees and qualifications, became a member of the Central Committee and effectively deputy in charge of the country. His brother Ilie leapt up the ladder of power to take control of the armed forces. His brother Floria was the leading journalist on the official newspaper *Scienteia.* His brother Ioan, also a member of the Central Committee, was Vice President of State Planning. His sisters did similarly well in politics, business and the health service. Nicu, Ceaucescu's son, was in charge of the Communist Youth Organization. He also preserved the family's reputation for alcoholism, and is still slowly dying of cirrhosis of the liver in prison. Nicu had a reputation as a rapist from the age of fourteen. Ceaucescu's daughter, Zoia, became a melancholy nymphomaniac. Corruption and prostitution reigned at the highest levels.

Ceaucescu decided that Rumania should repay its national debt. There was no reason for this other than it was one of his few ideas and it also was part of his simplistic nationalism that Rumania should not owe anybody any money. It was another idea he had picked up from Kim Il Sung. It meant that there was even less for the Rumanian people to eat, as it all had to be exported. In international dealings he was unsophisticated, mean and untrustworthy. Elena, who loved being received like a queen overseas, pressed Ceaucescu into obtaining an invitation to stay at Buckingham Palace. Ceaucescu dangled the carrot of a £300 million aircraft deal with the British to obtain this coveted photo-opportunity for the family collection and subsequently tried to pay for it not in cash as agreed, but with cloth and steel of dreadful quality from his polluting factories. When this was refused he offered ice cream, yoghurt and strawberries for the aircraft.

The Queen found the whole experience highly distasteful. Ceaucescu had grown obsessed with health and hygiene and arrived with a personal food taster and several bottles of alcohol with which he constantly sterilized his hands after shaking them with anybody. Ever since it was rumoured that Gheorghiu-Dej's cancer had been caused by radiation beamed at him by the Russians, Ceaucescu had ordered every room swept by Geiger counters before he set foot in them. Both he and Elena were terrified of germs and disease. If they had to shake hands with or, God forbid, kiss a child on a public appearance, the Securitate would select, disinfect and lock them up weeks beforehand. They drenched themselves in alcohol after the slightest human contact. After Fidel Castro had told Ceaucescu that he had uncovered a CIA plot to smear the inside of his clothes with poison that would make his hair fall out, Nicolae decided that it was unsafe to wear any of his clothes more than once. They became a priority State matter. The Securitate designed and made them all, keeping a year's hermetically sealed supply in a climate-controlled warehouse outside Bucharest. He took his own bed linen and basic foods everywhere. The Queen's staff were most surprised to find Ceaucescu and his vast entourage holding a conference in the Palace grounds at 6 a.m. Ceaucescu had naturally assumed that his rooms would be bugged.

Ceaucescu had a passion for eavesdropping, which he undertook with religious zeal, claiming that fear was the only way of creating an "honest population". Behind his office he had a personal monitoring room where he could select households

On official visits, Elena devoted herself to acquiring free gifts, honorary titles and diamonds. She even opened a "National Museum of Gifts to the Ceaucescus". Neither she nor Nicolae ever set foot in a shop or store, and officially were paid nothing. They simply accepted gifts from the State. Moreover, according to Pacepa, there was a slush fund with over $400 million in cash from Securitate operations. These included the selling of the Jewish population back to Israel at up to $50,000 a head and money from arms and, notoriously, drug smuggling. When they ran out of Jews, Ceaucescu tried to sell ethnic Germans back to their own country.

like TV channels. A new telephone was created capable of doubling up as a microphone. It became the only one available in Rumania. Televisions came with built-in transmitters. By 1980, every restaurant was equipped with ceramic ashtrays and vases stuffed full of listening devices. As the dissident Carol Kiraly said in 1984:

"The atmosphere of terror is beyond description. It permeates every aspect of everyday life. Distrust is so prevalent that no-one dares to communicate to anyone else . . ."

In spite of all this, the West still regarded him as an ally and sanctioned his absurd behaviour. As late as 1988, President Bush paid him an affectionate visit. Many leaders went hunting with him. He adored hunting, although he was a terrible shot and Securitate snipers were responsible for most of his hits.

His dogs were his other passion and he was very kind to them, taking good care that they weren't poisoned and generously giving them their own luxury villa complete with telephone and television. The motorcades of police-cars and bullet-proofed limousines that thundered through Bucharest often contained no-one other than Corbu, his favourite black labrador, riding in splendid isolation to the country.

The country was in an awful state. Animal feed was used in bread instead of flour. Petrol queues were two or three miles long. With no fuel people froze solid in temperatures of up to –30. The erratic gas supplies meant that fires would go off and come back on again, lethally unlit as people slept and then died by them. The whole population was suffering from acute depression; the suicide rate soared. Ceaucescu had banned contraception and abortion to increase the population. The birth rate rose by ninety-two per cent; the infant mortality rate by one hundred and forty-six per cent. There were no hospitals, doctors, nurses, milk and clothes to cope with the children. It was a cruel and ghastly blunder in social engineering. Still he persisted; women had to undergo monthly checks to ensure that they were not using contraceptive devices. AIDS, spread by contaminated blood and re-used needles, went unrecognized. The mentally handicapped, the unwanted children and the children of unwanted parents were dumped in remote hospitals to die of hepatitis and cholera. The industries that Ceaucescu established were appallingly ineffi-cient. Huge expense and time was devoted solely to managing his endless speeches and rallies. There were more absurd aspects to the horror. The regime had 20,000 Bibles sent to Rumania by a Christian organization secretly pulped into toilet paper which appeared with strange words like "Esau" "Jeremiah" and "God" still legible on it. A parrot, formerly a pet at one of the Ceaucescu households, was arrested by the Securitate after it was overheard saying "stupid Nicu", in reference to Ceaucescu's son. It was reputedly interrogated and throttled when it refused to disclose who had taught it the insult.

The final acts of megalomania were the "systematization" of the ancient, rural communities and his wanton destruction of old Bucharest to make his monolithic "House Of the People", one of the world's most boring buildings, a huge grey slab of concrete designed as a tribute to his own achievements. One of the largest buildings ever, this horror is now empty and decaying. It has no practical use at all. Icicles form in its hundreds of vast staterooms. The lighting and heating alone would take more power than all Bucharest's domestic users have at their disposal.

The "systematization" programme involved obliterating thousands of villages and moving the populations into "urban collectives" or "agro industrial complexes" where they would have to rent tiny flats on godless concrete estates. Sheer enslavement and vandalism, it was all part of Ceaucescu's distrust of the peasants and desire to put people where they could more easily be spied upon by himself and inform on each other. Elena thought that the new buildings would look much more tidy and clean than the old picturesque villages.

It was a Priest who eventually started the uprising in Rumania, in an incident unrelated to the upheavals elsewhere. Pastor Laszlos Tokes, who had been sent to remote Timisoara in disgrace for preaching sermons denouncing Ceaucescu, found himself continually harassed by the Securitate, who were frustrated in their desire to simply murder him by the international attention he had gained. In December 1989, the Securitate tried to evict him. His congregation, and then the whole town, resisted. The unrest spread. "You do not quieten your enemy by talking to him, but by burying him," screamed Ceaucescu at an emergency meeting. "Some few hooligans want to destroy Socialism and you make it child's play for them!"

Securitate were despatched to Timisoara with orders to kill. In the ensuing carnage and confusion there were reports of up to 60,000 dead, although after the revolution it was reduced to about one hundred with several hundred injured. Ceaucescu, still believing in his own god-like status as national saviour and genius, called for a huge rally to woo the people as he had done in 1968. He could not believe he was hated, and began to show signs of confusion and strain. His court sycophants humoured him and arranged a 100,000 strong rally on 21 December. It was a disaster. In front of the world's press his own people began to boo him, and he retreated in disbelief.

Dictators

The body of Nicolae Ceaucescu, photogaphed immediately after his execution on Christmas Eve, 1989. *Popperfoto*

Several of the army commanders, sensing which way the wind blew and with an eye on their future prospects, switched sides. Most importantly Generals Ilescu and Stanculescu, who had actually initiated the killing in Timisoara, suddenly transformed themselves into revolutionaries. General Milea was shot before he could defect, for failing to disperse the crowds. Ceaucescu went into hiding.

That night, as demonstrations finally erupted in the capital, the Securitate started shooting anything that moved. Using their huge web of tunnels under Bucharest to move about, they fought a bloody battle with the people and the army whilst other countries were celebrating Christmas. It only ended after the capture and execution of Ceaucescu, who incoherent and babbling with rage and disbelief had fled with Elena and their bodyguard by helicopter. Hearing news of proceedings in

Bucharest, their pilot cheerfully abandoned them on a lonely country road. Reduced to hitch-hiking, but with no idea of where they should go, they flagged down a local doctor who was driving past. In a bizarre last act, Elena held a gun to the man's head as he drove them aimlessly around, until he finally stopped in front of a police station. Their bodyguard disappeared. Resigned, but still refusing to believe that anything could happen to them, Nicolae and Elena gave themselves up.

They were wrong. A kangaroo court was quickly assembled and in a cynical trial worthy of his own regime they were condemned to death and shot. There were good reasons for wanting to dispose of them; it was felt that whilst they were alive the Securitate would not surrender, but more sinisterly, there were many army officers who were keen that Ceaucescu should not have the public opportunity to implicate them in his atrocities, not now the revolution had fallen into their hands. The Rumanians would still have to battle with Ceaucescu's former henchmen for their freedom.

There is an old Rumanian saying: "kiss the hand you cannot bite". It reflects a history of painful subservience to cruel masters. It was not only Ceaucescu's ego that created his hallucinatory bureaucracy of fear, but those who hoped to benefit from it, and even the people who submitted so completely for so long have some responsibility. Where strong rulers are favoured irrespective of their humanity, and wherever patriotism is a substitute for policies, democracy is a rapid casualty. Finally, that Nicolae Ceaucescu was admired and assisted by so many reputable leaders of the West may have been to their immediate political advantage; but it will endure to their eternal shame.

Chapter Six

Ivan the Terrible:
Sacrifices to Cronus

There are few stories in all history to compare with that of Ivan IV, The Terrible. Pious and depraved, majestic and bestial, Ivan is a tragic figure. He embodied the contradictory impulses of his society; a devout Christianity in which Russia was to be the last, and greatest Rome, and a terrible, dark worship of destruction.

Cronus is the ancient pagan father of the gods. He is Time itself, and devours his own children. Late in his life, Ivan confessed to secretly worshipping this shadowy deity. Referring to his beloved wife, Anastasia, who died of suspected poisoning before his abdication, he wrote to the aristocrats, "If you had not taken her from me, there would have been no sacrifices to Cronus."

This self-portrait of a dark God-of-Wrath, consuming his subjects in revenge and anger, echoes the words of a prophecy said to have been made on his birth. Far away from Moscow, in the Tartar stronghold of Kazan, which was to be the scene of his greatest triumph, the wife of the ruling Khan had a strange premonition. She called the Russian envoy to her and said: "A Tsar is born among you; two teeth has he. With one he shall devour us; but with the other, you."

Ivan was crowned Prince in the Cathedral of the Assumption at the age of three and a half. His father Vasily III died on 3 December. Earlier in the year, an inconspicuous purple mark had appeared on Vasily's thigh. This refused to go away, and turned into a boil. In September, the boil suppurated, swelling up with oozing pus. Vasily was barely able to walk, and rapidly

Ivan IV, Tsar of Russia. *Hulton-Deutsch*

moved to secure the throne for his tiny son. He set up a Regency Council to rule during Ivan's childhood, and obliged the Boyars, Russia's aristocrats, to swear allegiance to Ivan.

The boil became a huge abscess; the pus "filled a basin". A core, one and a half inches wide, came out. Vasily recovered briefly, but when gangrene followed along with a putrefying stench, he died of blood poisoning.

Ivan inherited a country equivalent to France, Spain, Britain and Italy in size. In spite of its enormity, it hardly appeared on a map. Explorers firmly expected to find China battened onto the eastern side of Europe. The huge plains and wastes of Russia had only ten to twelve million inhabitants in total, less than the number that died under Stalin in the 1930s. Most were peasants, many in conditions of serfdom that was little more than slavery. The peasants were further crushed by taxes.

The Russians were a tough, stocky race, with fashionable beards and big bellies, a passion for alcohol and celebration, and a reputation for sodomy. The prevalence of the latter amazed foreigners, who reported that they do it "not only with boys but with men and horses". A popular Russian curse was "may a dog defile your mother". Women were habitually beaten by their husbands, as the saying went: "if a woman be not beaten with the whip once a week, she will not be good . . ." Torture was legal. Women convicted of killing their husbands were buried alive; counterfeiters had molten lead poured down their throats. Only spoken evidence was necessary for conviction, but as this was, above all, a religious society, witnesses first kissed the Cross. This was the most serious action this people could perform; their souls were in peril if they lied.

The Russian Orthodox Church saw itself as the last bastion of true Christianity. All other Churches and faiths were heretical. Foreigners, particularly Catholics and Jews, were regarded with acute suspicion, as potential carriers of some other doctrine which might sweep through the country like a disease. All movements of the population were restricted, and foreign travel without permission was punishable by death ". . . so that the people may learn nothing about foreign lands . . ." It was a situation similar to Stalin's Russia, with the Church in the place of the Communist Party. It was a vast, wealthy and powerful organization, with a Messianic mission as successor to the Christian Empires of Rome and Constantinople. A monk had prophesied to Ivan's father: ". . . the ruler of the present Orthodox Empire is on Earth the sole Emperor of the Christians . . . two Romes have fallen, but the third stands and a fourth there shall not be . . ."

According to Ivan's fabricated family tree he was descended from the Roman Emperor Augustus himself. The symbolic importance of his position placed a suffocating burden on the young Ivan.

Acclaimed publicly as a virtual god, and privately abused and ignored by his ministers, Ivan's childhood was spent in shadows and fear. Later he wrote that no-one gave him ". . . any loving care . . . everything I experienced was unbefitting my tender years . . ." When not trussed up in the stifling uniform of a prince, he was treated like a beggar. He flitted through the inky, labyrinthine corridors and chambers of the Kremlin, a frightened creature, nursing distrust and revenge in his blackening heart.

Ivan's mother, Elena, made her own bid for the throne. The Regency Council disintegrated as its members were imprisoned and exiled. Elena was not a bad ruler, but not a good mother. In 1538, four years after she took power, she was poisoned. Ivan was left utterly alone in the world. The Boyars, and their governing body, the Duma, who had sworn to his father to protect and support him, quarrelled and fought over power they now considered theirs. The Tartars took advantage of bitter in-fighting to invade, burning monasteries, raping and dismembering nuns and monks. Meanwhile Ivan, aged twelve and developing a savage and morbid temperament, had taken to throwing dogs off the Kremlin battlements "to observe their pain and convulsions".

There was clearly something violent in the air. At the age of fourteen, he gathered together a teenage gang and roamed the streets of Moscow, exorcizing his anger and frustration by mugging innocent pedestrians. Increasingly, he confided in the Metropolitan Makary, the leader of the Orthodox Church, and Ivan Vorontsov, a member of the old Moscow gentry. After Prince Andrey Shuisky, a member of the dominant Boyar family, broke in on a meeting of the three and tried to kill Vorontsov in front of him, he asserted his position and had Shuisky thrown to the dogs.

At sixteen he told the Duma that he intended to marry, and that furthermore, he would take the title of Tsar, equivalent to Emperor, or Caesar. It also resembled the Tartar title of Khan, meaning "A king that giveth not tribute to any man". His mother had Tartar ancestors; in Ivan the blood of both Christian Russian autocrats and their bitter enemies, the pagan Mongol emperors, flowed together. The Duma were astonished at the maturity of his speech. His budding cruelty was matched by unsurpassed intelligence. In January 1547, he was crowned Tsar and Autocrat of All Russia.

He married Anastasia Romanovna, who came from an untitled but loyal Boyar family. The older aristocracy felt snubbed by this, regarding her as an upstart commoner. Her descendants, the Romanovs, were still ruling three hundred and fifty years later, when the Revolution came and the Bolsheviks wiped them out. After his wedding, Ivan made the first of many penitential pilgrimages, covering over forty miles on foot in the bitter Winter cold.

The country was in a troubled state. The aristocratic Glinsky family had now become the lords of misrule. The population resorted to arson to express their despair. They appealed to Ivan in vain; he toyed with them, singeing the beards of petitioners and splashing them with boiling wine. In June, a fire gutted the heart of Moscow, killing thousands. The mob confronted Ivan, who woke up to his awesome responsibility, and began to govern.

He had a reputation for intellectual brilliance, but by his own admission was also wild and cruel. He was aware that he needed good advice, and surrounded himself with a "Chosen Council".

Priestly figures often exerted great influence at the Russian court. The Rasputin of Ivan's day was a monk named Sylvester; who dazzled Ivan with his stories of ghosts and miracles, "scaring me with bogies", as Ivan later described it. Significantly Ivan was also influenced by the theories of a pamphleteer called Peresvetov. This man was a much travelled mercenary, who referred in his writing to the occult wisdom contained in a book he called the *Secreta Secretorum*. This book, which Ivan had in his Palace Library, supposedly contained the secret advice given by Aristotle to Alexander the Great. The Turkish Emperor Mehmet had learned a philosophy of terror from it, and swept away all who opposed his reforms. The book urged rulers to inspire awe in their subjects; to be remote and distrustful and to test the loyalty of nobles by seeing "what each will suffer on your account". Those who wished to be absolute rulers should not be afraid of shedding blood; it was the only reputation worth having.

Ivan started off trying to reform the land-laws, and proposing reforms in taxation and the system of justice to benefit the peasants. He cursed the Boyars for their treatment of him as a child. "Usurious bloodsuckers", he called them. They looked down at their feet, nervously apologizing. His reforms soon ran up against their interests, however. Ivan desperately needed to have land that he could reward people with for loyalty. But thirty per cent of all arable land was owned by the Church, the Russian real-estate moguls, who were opposed to any reforms which might affect their vast wealth. The Church was a notoriously tough bank and building society, always eager to re-possess property. Life in the cloisters had become opulent and corrupt; the Church had little time for charity, and took badly to Ivan's attempts to make it liable for tax or to make it set up poor-houses.

His other policy was to wage war. In 1552, at the age of twenty-two his army took the fortified Tartar city of Kazan and massacred the cream of the Tartar nobility. This was an historic victory over Russia's old enemies, and afterwards the Russian people gave him the title of "Terrible", to indicate the awesome stature he had acquired.

Ivan fell ill after Kazan. His fever was not thought to be pure coincidence; his reforms had not been popular with the Boyars. Now, as he lay on what many thought was his deathbed, he asked the Boyars to swear allegiance to his infant son, Dimitry, just as his own father had done. In spite of his stature, they would not "serve a babe". Hailed as a hero one minute, Ivan discovered how little he could trust even his closest allies. Rallying his strength, he manipulated his loyal forces from his sickbed and succeeded in crushing the rebellion.

In the ten years that followed, Russia became the region's greatest power, but afterwards became locked into an endless, draining and failed war to conquer the Baltic. English traders, looking for China, found their way to Russia, and an erratic relationship began between the two monarchs, Ivan and Elizabeth.

The English merchants saw Ivan at the height of his reign, enthroned in splendour, encrusted with jewels and crossing himself before each of his frequent mouthfuls of food and drink; "He setteth his whole delight upon two things. First to serve God, as undoubtedly he is very devout in his religion, and the second, how to subdue and conquer his enemies."

Despite riding high on conquest and initiating reforms which improved the peasants' lot, Ivan was increasingly cynical and debauched. He drank furiously and having decided that no-one was trustworthy surrounded himself with sycophants, from whom he expected nothing but shallowness. They kissed his hands and feet, flattering and soothing him. He developed an addiction to masked balls and theatrical executions. He was promiscuous with both sexes. Criticism was unwelcome. Dmitry Obolensky, a Prince, reproached the son of one of Ivan's generals for his homosexual relationship with Ivan. Dmitry was invited down into Ivan's cellars to select a favourite vintage and hacked to death among the casks.

The stalemate of the Baltic Wars angered Ivan, who detected a plot. He slew one of his princes with a mace, and accused his prize general, Kurbsky, of treason. Kurbsky saw the shadow of Ivan reaching out to touch him and deserted, denouncing Ivan for "torturing his subjects with red-hot pincers and needles driven under the nails . . ." Ivan compelled the messenger who brought Kurbsky's letter to read it aloud whilst Ivan drove the iron point of his staff through his foot into the floor. It was the first instalment of a bizarre correspondence these two entered into. In long angry letters to Kurbsky, who in exile became an unwilling confidant, Ivan revealed an exceptional literary talent, and the soul of a man who resented the position his fate had thrust upon him.

His personality was driven and obsessive, eating up the world around him. But the full potential of his latent cruelty and bitterness was restrained by his wife, Anastasia. They had already shared in the tragedy of his first son's death. Dimitry had drowned when his nurse accidentally dropped him in a river. Since then she had borne him another five children, but only a couple, Ivan Ivanovitch and his brother, the imbecilic Theodore, survived beyond the age of two. Ivan called his wife his "little heifer", and she was regarded with universal love by the Russian people. She was beautiful, wise and graceful, and ". . . bore no malice towards anyone". Her decline and death in 1560, when Ivan was still not quite thirty years old, brought about a distinct change in his personality. Impatience became anger, suspicion deepened into paranoia. Casual cruelty grew into a need for daily sadism. Ivan distanced himself from his former advisers, and in the words of one contemporary "lived in great danger and fear of treason which he daily discovered, and spent much time in the examination, torturing and execution of his subjects . . ."

Amidst growing dissent, he began to toy with the idea of abdication. At the end of 1564, hundreds of sleds began to cart off tons of treasure and icons from the palace and treasury to

Dictators

Sloboda, a hunting lodge sixty miles from Moscow. This was transformed into a fortified camp. Nobody had the faintest idea what Ivan was up to. They watched, mystified. Then, without disclosing his intentions to anybody, and designating no heir, he slipped out of Moscow and left the nation leaderless. In a letter read out to the Boyars by a messenger on 3 January 1565, he bitterly accused the Church and Government of corruption, treason and responsibility for all his personal troubles, past and present and wallowed in melodramatic self-pity: "Wherefore the Tsar and Grand Prince not wishing to endure these many acts of treachery, has abandoned the Tsardom with a heavy heart and now travels wheresoever God may lead him . . ."

The peasants feared they might have lost a champion. A popular uprising was on the cards; anarchy loomed. The foreign powers on the borders licked their lips.

The Duma humbled itself, and despatched the Archbishop of Novgorod to plead with Ivan. Without Ivan, they were "poor and inconsolable sheep . . . without a shepherd, and the wolves, our enemies surround us . . ." If he returned, he could "punish traitors at his own discretion". Ivan categorically refused to resume his position. He wanted more than that.

When he returned to Moscow in February, still only thirty-five years old, most of his hair had fallen out; his eyes were curiously glazed. After four weeks of negotiation, he had been granted absolute power over the life and property of any disobedient subject. A part of the nation was to be set aside for him, existing only to further his will, staffed and run by his hand-picked personnel. This part of Muscovy was to be called the "Oprichina" – the "widow's portion", reflecting his continuing self-pity. The Oprichina initially consisted of twenty towns and their surroundings. Ivan expanded it to include over a third of the entire Empire. His intention was plain: to undermine and destroy the hereditary aristocracy he so feared and blamed for his childhood misery and the obstruction of his authority. The rest of Russia was left to the former administration, with Ivan presiding over everything.

He now possessed power the pharaohs would have envied. Those he employed to staff and run his personal Empire had only one thing in common; they had to swear complete and unquestioning obedience to Ivan in all things: "He that loveth father or mother more than me is not worthy of me; and he that loveth son or daughter more is not worthy of me . . ."

Ivan's revenge began immediately. No specific charges were necessary for the deaths that followed, though generally a vague accusation would be made that so-and-so had done, or plotted, or thought "all manner of evil things". Ivan showed no gratitude for past services; the hero of Kazan, Prince Gorbaty, along with his adolescent son were executed, as well as countless lesser nobles. Some faced death bravely, protesting their innocence. One Dmitri Sheyev "sang all day from memory the canon to our Lord Jesus Christ" as he was slowly impaled on a stake. An English merchant arrived in Moscow in 1566, just in time to catch the fall-out: "This Emperor of Moscovia hath used lately great cruelty towards his nobility and gentlemen, by putting to death, whipping and banishing above 400 . . . one worried with bears, of another he cut off his nose, tongue, his ears and his lips, the third he set upon a pole . . ."

When Ivan discovered a real plot a year later, the carnage extended beyond the immediate suspects and their families. The Oprichniki rode around Moscow for days armed with axes, chopping down whosoever they chanced upon. One Boyar, discovered hiding in a monastery, had needles driven under his nails before he was roasted alive in a large pan. Moscow was not the place to be. The English Ambassador, negotiating between Ivan and Elizabeth, wrote anxiously to his Queen: "Of late the Tsar hath beheaded no small number of his nobility . . . causing their heads to be laid in the streets to see who dares to mourn them . . . I intend to see him so soon as I can . . . the sooner to be out of his country where heads go so fast to the pot."

Ivan, who had annexed a whole suburb of Moscow for his personal use, spent most of his time at the fortress town of Sloboda, indulging simultaneously in his twin pleasures of

> Ivan's servants, from all social classes, including
> aristocrats, were called the Oprichniki. They looked
> and behaved like the Devil's own slaves. Dressed in
> black, riding black horses, with a strange, ever-present
> insignia of a dog and broom, they were forbidden any
> contact with the normal citizens and developed their
> own customs and religious rites. They were the model
> in eeriness and brutality for Hitler's SS.

religion and depravity. One brought on a craving for the other.
It was a strict regime. There were several church services each
day, commencing at 3 a.m., and after each he would make
frequent excursions to the dungeons to gratify the desire for
torture that worship aroused in him. Here he was described as
"never so happy in countenance and speech": "Blood often
splashes in his face, but he does not mind; indeed he is
delighted, and to indicate his joy, he shouts 'Hoyda! Hoyda!'"

Occasionally there were large-scale entertainments, as when
he had several hundred beggars drowned in a lake, or fed
rebellious friars to wild animals, or sewed enemies up in
bearskins and threw them to the dogs. At other times, Ivan
would beat himself, pounding his own forehead on the ground
until it turned black with bruises and ran red with blood.

Russia's now disastrous wars in the Baltic laid an enormous
burden of taxation on the people. Ivan, who had managed to
maintain a trading agreement with England, looked to Elizabeth
for weapons and a possible alliance and refuge in case unrest
should force him to flee. Elizabeth would not be drawn into
Ivan's wars, and although she offered Ivan refuge, she declined
his reciprocal offer of shielding her from her own subjects,
which offended Ivan. She did supply him with weapons, to the
consternation of the Polish King, Sigismund, who told her that
Ivan was the ". . . hereditary foe of all free nations . . . he maketh
himself strong to vanquish all others". She also obstructed his

efforts to marry into the English royal family; Ivan had become inflamed with passion at the thought of some youthful English flesh; he already claimed to have deflowered a thousand Russian virgins.

After Anastasia's death he had made a political marriage to a Tartar princess, Maria, who had a reputation for cruelty. When she was poisoned by a nasty fish supper in 1569, Prince Staritsky, one of the Boyars who ran what little was left of Russia, was convicted on the evidence of a cook. Ivan compelled Staritsky to drink poison, and murdered his entire family; even his mother was strangled. The cook, the cook's sons, the fishmonger who sold the offending fish, and even the fisherman who caught it were all executed along with their families. Two years later, Ivan's third wife, Marfa also died of poisoning.

It was in this year, 1569, that Ivan staged his most spectacular massacres, at Novgorod and Pskov. Novgorod was virtually on the border with warring Lithuania, and a prime target for Ivan's paranoia. When a disreputable source suggested that these cities were planning treason, Ivan moved an army of 15,000 Oprichniki northwards, in great secrecy. In order to maintain surprise they killed anyone who crossed their path, and by 2 January 1571, they reached the outskirts of Novgorod. The Oprichniki ominously sealed up all exits and refuges. Having denounced the

---

The old accounts of the slaughter give the number of victims as 60,000, with the killing continuing for five weeks. The occupants, irrespective of age or sex, were hanged, flayed, beheaded, impaled or thrown off the bridge. Ivan built a chute into the Volkhov river, and slid the still-breathing remains of his torture-victims down in to the shallows. There the Oprichniki waded in their boots, hacking and stabbing and gouging. The river turned red.

Dictators

Archbishop as "a thief, traitor, murderer and a wolf", Ivan went to church to get himself in the right frame of mind for the ensuing sport, praying with particular intensity during the service. Afterwards, he repaired to the Archbishop's residence for a spot of supper. As he began to eat, the massacre began.

Just when death seemed certain for everybody, Ivan decided to pardon the survivors, and requesting them to wish him a long and happy reign, he moved on to Pskov. There the population suffered a similar fate, and were only spared extinction by the intervention of a "Holy Fool", who foresaw Ivan's death if the killing continued. Ivan remained susceptible to prophecies.

That Winter, Russia suffered a terrible famine, with the peasants resorting to cannibalism to stave off starvation. Many of Ivan's victims were put to practical use. After the famine came plague. To cap Russia's misery, in Summer the Tartars invaded from the south and swept into Moscow.

Ivan had been preoccupied with torturing a couple of old enemies when the Tartars attacked. He had devised an ingenious death for one suspected opponent, Nikita Funikov, whom the Oprichniki had doused with alternately boiling and freezing water until his skin literally peeled off. It made an interesting change from flaying. Learning of the invasion, he made for Novgorod, where he planned to take a ship for England along with four hundred and fifty tons of treasure he had dragged along with him. Having been deprived of what he felt to be rightfully his in his youth, he had now become an insatiable plunderer.

The Tartars set fire to Moscow, and then surrounded and cut down any trying to escape the flames. Half the population died, as many as half a million people.

The English observers were rather smug about this latest catastrophe, calling it the "just punishment of God on such a wicked nation", and concluding that the Russians had been destroyed because of their fondness for sodomy. They also observed that what with his own cruelty and the famines, plagues and Tartars, "the Tsar hath but few people left".

Ivan the Terrible murdered his own son but remorse drove him mad. This painting by Rjepin shows the demented dictator embracing his dead son. *Hulton-Deutsch*

Dictators

The Tartars were defeated at the battle of Molodi, after which the Oprichina was slowly re-integrated back into the state, and the thugs disbanded. The organization disintegrated through sheer exhaustion. Moreover, there was little left in Russia worth fighting over.

Ivan survived for another decade, presiding over the collapse of the Russian Empire he had taken to such heights. His cruelty did not abate, though the scale diminished. His experiments with terror and debauchery left him shattered. His attempt to create a new class based on loyalty alone failed. He was feared, hated, but could not command loyalty without purchasing it. Russia was demoralized and poor, plunged into pagan medieval gloom. While the rest of Europe basked in the light of the Renaissance, the figure of Cronus still ruled in the shadows of Russia. Out of 34,000 settlements recorded in Russia at the end of his reign, eighty-three per cent were deserted. On 14 November 1581, Ivan upbraided his daughter-in-law Elena, who was pregnant, about her clothes. Ivanovitch intervened, and Ivan drove the spike on his iron-tipped staff into his son's head. The wound festered and he died a few days later. He had been the one surviving hope of the people, although he shared in many of Ivan's vices.

Ivan went insane with grief, tearing his hair and crying for nights without end. He began to dispense his hoarded wealth to the monasteries, ordering that they pray for his son every day. He also drew up a list of the victims of his terror whom he wished the clergy to pray for, displaying an amazing memory for names. From Novgorod alone he listed 1,500 men and their wives and families. The countless unknown were to be acknowledged by the constant sad refrain: "as to their names, O Lord, you know them . . ."

In 1583 he started suffering acutely from a condition rather like arthritis, which resulted in the rapid deterioration of his joints. Horribly, the vertebrae of his very spine fused solid. He was bent nearly double. In January 1584 he began to rot on his feet; in the words of an English merchant: "The Emperor began to swell grievously in his coddes, with which he had much offended above fifty years, boasting of a thousand virgins he had deflowered . . ."

His body putrified internally. Ivan sat, playing chess and doting on his treasure, regretting that he would have to leave it. Sixty Lapland witches were imported to predict the precise moment of death. After consultation they came up with 18 March.

Ivan improved. He even took guests on an extraordinary tour of his treasury, where he lectured them on the occult properties of his jewels and used them in front of his amazed audience to confirm his impending demise.

On 18 March, to general consternation, Ivan rose up healthy and cheerful. The witches remained confident. Later Ivan leapt out of a relaxing bath, sat down for a game of chess and at last fell over dead.

Russia was left to his idiot son Theodore, civil war and destruction at the hands of the Polish and Tartar armies.

Chapter Seven

Emperor Bokassa I: The Napoleon of Bangui

Jean Bedel Bokassa, President and self-styled Emperor of the Central African Republic, had an expensive obsession with French history. The former French colony that he ruled is one of the poorest countries in the world. Its total budget in 1977 was $70 million, about the annual turnover of the largest branch of a major supermarket. Bokassa contrived to spend a third of this on his coronation as Emperor Bokassa I. It was a memorable forty-eight hours.

The ceremony faithfully replicated the coronation of his favourite historical figure, Napoleon Bonaparte, and the attention paid to detail in this orgy of spending is staggering. The short, squat, ugly Emperor wore an ankle-length tunic of velvet and shoes of pearls. The Imperial mantle was embroidered with gold bees, precisely like Napoleon's. Everywhere, two golden laurel fronds bracketed the gold initial "B" for Bokassa, replacing the "N" of Napoleon. He trailed behind him a thirty-foot, crimson-velvet, gold-embroidered and ermine-trimmed mantle weighing over seventy pounds. He was weighed down by a jewel-encrusted, gold-hilted sword and ebony staff of office. The heavy crown was also an exact replica of Napoleon's, fronted with the golden French Imperial eagle. The throne, covered with more red velvet, trimmed with gold, was backed by another vast gold eagle, whose outspread wings threw an appropriate shadow over the Emperor and his Empress Catherine, formerly plain Mrs Bokassa, a peasant girl from the same mud-hut village as the Emperor.

The Emperor was conveyed through the dusty tracks of the

Emperor Bokassa I: The Napoleon of Bangui

The coronation of "Emperor" Bokassa. *Hulton-Deutsch*

capital, Bangui, to his coronation in a gilded coach drawn by eight white imported Normandy horses. Fourteen had been sent from France but the rest had died in the heat. His raggle-taggle army lined the route, cheering fitfully. Bokassa, who had warmed up by spending several days watching films of Queen Elizabeth's coronation, gave a much practised royal wave with his white-gloved hand. Even the church had been re-titled Notre Dame de Bangui for the occasion.

> The cannibalism stories that emerged during and after
> his overthrow received a boost from the discoveries
> made at his Royal Palace, where it seems he had been
> butchering children and allegedly feeding the bits he
> couldn't manage to his four pet crocodiles. In some
> lurid accounts the bodies of up to forty of them were
> found at the bottom of his swimming pool, with
> another dozen in the cold-storage room, left over from
> the feasting of the previous night. There is one question
> that springs to mind in reading these extraordinary
> claims: if he ate them, who cooked them? Who was
> Bokassa's chef? Was he French?

Over 2,500 guests attended from all over the world. Many
more had been invited, including every European leader and
monarch. Most had politely returned their gold-edged
invitations. The British were rude, the Americans cut off aid. Of
those international dignitaries who came, six hundred had been
lodged for several days in the best hotels or in specially
constructed housing, fed and watered in Imperial style at the
country's expense. The French had provided Bokassa with $2.5
million worth of credit to purchase a fleet of Mercedes
limousines to ferry his guests about in, and to provide a
ceremonial escort of two hundred BMW motorcycles.

After the ceremony, at which Bokassa solemnly promised to
continue "the democratic evolution of the Empire", 4,000 guests
sat down to a full, French style banquet at the Renaissance
Palace in Bangui. There, to the strains of a French Naval Band,
the Emperor and Empress waltzed the night away, clad in
elegant Parisian evening dress.

When Bokassa's regime blossomed from tyranny and bad taste
into open horror a couple of years later, an appalling but

compelling sub-plot to this parody was rumoured. As part of his coronation celebrations, Bokassa had ordered that conditions for a number of political prisoners be made more lenient. They were taken out of chains, and given decent food and exercise. They were told that after the ceremony they would receive an Imperial pardon. In fact, having been suitably fed up, it is claimed, they were expertly diced and served to the guests in coronation sauce of Parisian richness.

The story, however speculative, has distinct echoes of classical tragedy; a false Emperor begins his reign with an accursed banquet at which, in eating his victims, the guests symbolically share in his crimes. It would be convenient to simply consider the Bokassas of history as evil incarnate, occurring in spite of the best efforts of others, but their stories show nothing so straightforward. Their creation involves a mechanism as complex and far-reaching as the stock market; responsibility – and guilt – for the final debacle is shared by all who expected to profit.

Like Idi Amin in Uganda, Jean Bedel Bokassa was the worst possible publicity for an African nation struggling to be taken seriously; an unfortunate mutant prodigy of the colonial past. The Imperial ceremony was both a way of flattering the French, and a means of announcing that he had inherited their mantle of absolute rule and was above the rest of his nation.

The rest of his Empire consisted of a central portion of Equatorial Africa which, though nearly as large as France itself, has a tiny population of around two and a half million, forty per cent of whom are under the age of fifteen. In some areas there is less than one person per seven hundred and forty-one acres. The population is largely tribal, and frequently nomadic, which contributes to the lack of a single national identity. Westerners trying to connect the Central African Republic with anything other than the excesses of Bokassa will probably come up with the image of naked pygmies with huge lip plugs being pursued through steaming jungle by roaring lions. It is Bongo Bongo land of Western prejudice, the homeland of African stereotypes,

Dictators

> There was no Central African Republic before the French came into Equatorial Africa at the turn of the century. The area, remote and unexplored, had been the location of a number of mythical kingdoms, including that of Prester John, the legendary Christian Emperor of Ethiopia. In the sixteenth century, the Portuguese had invaded, lured by these fabulous stories and looking for gold, without success. In the next century, the Arabs, sweeping down from the north found it, in the shape of "black gold" as slaves were known. The African tribes, originally quite populous, were decimated by the slave trade and the smallpox, measles and syphilis that came with it. Slaves were Africa's major wealth, and were rapaciously mined like a precious ore.

showing not only our own ignorance, but also what an artificial, haphazard creation the country is.

When the French moved into the area it was known as Ubangi-Shari, and from 1920, it was a full-scale colony. The French leased fifty per cent of the country to a mere seventeen French companies, who were given free rein to exploit the labour and natural products. These used enforced labour, torture and hostage – forcing the population to collect the increasingly rare but precious natural rubber vine. In 1927, a local leader, Chief Mindogon, was whipped to death by the territorial guards of one French company, because he had failed to supply enough rubber-collectors. He was the father of Jean Bedel Bokassa, then aged six.

After World War II, in which many Africans served their French masters courageously, President de Gaulle sought to retain a more subtle grip over the African colonies. They were offered two choices: remain willingly as extensions of France, subject to French rule but also French assistance, or take complete independence. The fear of Barthelmy Boganda, then French-appointed ruler of Ubangi-Shari, was that now the colonial powers had divided Equatorial Africa up into a system of small states, if they took independence, Ubangi-Shari would definitely be drawing the short straw. It was now, by comparison with its neighbours, a small and insignificant province which could expect to be trampled on. And while the French could withdraw their troops and administrators, their businessmen still had a firm grip on the sources of the country's meagre wealth. This state was not yet a nation. It had never had a central authority, such as an independent government; it had always been a loose collection of tribes. It needed help to make the transition.

There were no compromises available, and in 1960, the Central African Republic was born. It was a reluctant independence, a nation that was forced into being. Barthelmy, the only man with sufficient wisdom and stature to solve the nation's dilemmas, died in an unexplained aircraft crash. He was succeeded by David Dacko, and five years of increasing corruption and chaos followed, before on 31 December 1965, Bokassa seized power.

Bokassa was raised in a French Catholic Mission and joined the French army at the earliest possible opportunity. By 1965, then forty-four years old, he had served in French Indochina, and risen to the rank of lieutenant, impressing with his loyalty and obvious fascination for French military history. He claimed to be the nephew of Barthelmy Boganda, thus giving him a vague, tribal right to the position of national leader. He became a member of Dacko's Government after leaving the French army, and used his French contacts and influence to acquire the position of Chief of Staff at the Ministry of Defence.

His coup was a surprise for the French. Although the country was officially independent, they reserved the right to interfere when necessary. The unrest of Dacko's regime had made them fear for their business and strategic interests in the country; they were worried about the possibility of a Marxist-led, popular uprising. They had been planning their own coup, and were out-manoeuvred by Bokassa, who learned about their intentions and arrested the chosen replacement to Dacko on New Year's Eve. A few hours later, troops loyal to Bokassa, many of whom had served with him in the French army, overran Bangui. Dacko handed over the combination of the safe to Bokassa, and went into exile in Paris.

Until that extraordinary coronation twelve years later, there was little to distinguish Bokassa's Government from any other confused, violent and corrupt post-colonial regime. It was run on the simple maxim of "to the victors, the spoils". Bokassa abolished any vestiges of democracy, making himself President and head of the armed forces, the Ministry of Information and Minister for Justice. Like Amin, he appointed people from his own tribal background to ministerial positions, and, like Amin, he regularly shot them. The army officers who had supported him were rewarded with vast salary increases and promotions. Towards the public, he behaved initially like a benign tribal chieftain, making extravagant public gestures to compensate for his inability to govern. He donated his first month's salary towards the building of a hospital, and even paid in cash one or two of the country's outstanding bills. Work was started on a public transport system; a central market was built. To a population thoroughly accustomed to mere exploitation, these were definite signs of improvement, which predictably, were not sustained.

France didn't care for military leaders who took charge without first obtaining permission from them. However, Bokassa's regime was preferable to the Communism they dreaded, and the man was such a Francophile, it was touching. He never renounced his French citizenship and idolized De Gaulle. The death of his father as a result of French colonialism only seemed to have filled him with superstitious admiration for their power, and gratitude to the French Church and Army for taking the position of surrogate parent. He regarded de Gaulle's successor, Giscard d'Estaing, as his "cousin". The country was still financially dependent on France, which was the outlet for half its exports and from whom it received vast amounts of aid, up to $20 million a year. However, nearly ninety per cent of that aid was "bi-lateral", that is, it involved some return concession from the Central African Republic; the more aid it provided, the bigger France's financial interest in the country, and effectively in Bokassa became. The country was better off as an outright colony. Within a few years of taking power, Bokassa persuaded the French to send a small contingent of paratroopers to guarantee the stability of his regime. The original group of eighty quickly swelled until by 1969, twenty per cent of the armed forces were French. Bokassa was not particular about where his money came from, however, and at various times the United States, the Soviet Union, Yugoslavia, Rumania and South Africa were all involved in "projects".

The thin line that existed between Bokassa's private bank account and that of the Government was removed when his Minister of Finance, Colonel Alexandra Banza, was arrested, tortured and executed in 1969. Banza, something of an anomaly, had foolishly attempted to restrict the tide of personal enrichment. From then on, Bokassa began a process of what he termed "privatization" of state assets and revenue. This meant that the diamond and uranium mining interests which were the most desirable of the country's assets became the property of a handful of closely related people, with French companies owning the mining concessions. These accounted for fifty per cent of the country's exports. Bokassa had shares in every national business, and a complete monopoly on internal trade. By bribery and fear he completely subjugated the whole civil service to his will. There were 4,000 Government officials, but few bothered to do any work, and even fewer had any power. They lived in the old colonial villas and clubs, desperately aping their former French rulers. The country was only saved from bankruptcy because its currency was still the French franc, and France protected its value. It was a profoundly sad situation.

Dictators

Bokassa made himself President for life in 1972. There was always a plot in the offing somewhere, but they became a regular, bi-annual event in the following years, generally launched by those who were jealous of the success of Bokassa's "privatization" and wanted a piece of the action. He was desperately attached to even the most meagre portion of the fortune he had amassed. In 1973, after an attempted robbery at his palace he became crazed with anger at the idea of being stolen from and personally beat to death three convicted thieves being held in a nearby prison. They had absolutely nothing to do with the failed burglary, but he had long before ceased to regard the populace as individuals, rather than a squirming mass of limbs to be hacked at. The following day he passed a decree sanctifying property, with ears and limbs to be cut off for the most minor theft.

He now had annexed the major portion of his country's wealth, and showered it on visiting diplomats. Giscard d'Estaing made a trip in 1975, and was greeted by a handful of diamonds and taken on hunting trips to Bokassa's personal game reserve, which took up most of the eastern half of the country.

Bokassa, now an established alcoholic, announced his intention to become Emperor in 1976, and started building himself a palace at Berengo. This was not yet finished at the time of his coronation. It was to have landscaped lawns, swimming pools, fountains, bullet-proof glass and fortress-like defences. The cost of this, added to his absurd coronation, devastated the nation's finances. No one could curb him, and a year later he announced yet more publicly financed celebrations to commemorate the anniversary of his coronation. The Government ran out of money, and was unable to pay any of its civil servant salaries or any student grants. In January 1979, Bokassa decreed that all schoolchildren had to purchase and wear ludicrous, French-style uniforms, the sole manufacturer of which was an establishment owned by his wife. As most of the schoolchildren of Bangui had no books, and many went barefoot, it was not a practical or popular decision. Bokassa was being quite serious, and students found themselves turned away from school for being incorrectly dressed. General unrest spread, and a certain amount of looting began in the town centre. The army were sent in and gunned down one hundred and fifty to two hundred disruptive students and children. Bokassa blamed it all on the Russians and denounced the "stupid" Government decree about school uniforms; as Emperor, he would overrule it and make sure that whoever was responsible was punished. The French bailed out the country, and civil service salaries were raised by fifty per cent to keep them quiet.

In April, Bokassa arrested a number of students and teachers for circulating leaflets denouncing his wealth. Strikes and "sit-ins" began. Between 18 and 20 April, the "Imperial Guard" rounded up one hundred students and children and took them to Ngaragbo prison. In the days that followed they were systematically beaten to death in the presence of, and with the active participation of Bokassa. Their bodies were then secretly buried. This was in the Internationai Year of the Child.

The French were now horribly embarrassed by the stories coming out of Bangui. Stalling for time, they set up an African Mission Of Inquiry with representatives from five other African States to investigate the allegations. In the meantime, they tried desperately to get rid of Bokassa before the inquiry could find him guilty, and put them in the position of being the principal sponsors of a mass-murderer. Their efforts were in vain, Bokassa refused all their invitations to take trips outside his own country, and stayed in his fortified palace.

The inquiry found him guilty in August 1979. In September, because of the sanctions his barbarous behaviour had earned for his country, Bokassa was forced to take his begging bowl to that banker to the criminally insane, Colonel Gaddafi of Libya. Whilst he was out of the country, the French launched "Operation Barracuda", and in a bloodless coup dragged David Dacko out of bed in Paris and thrust him, still half-asleep, back into the Presidential Palace in Bangui. Bokassa found himself stranded in Libya, which is a kind of rest-home for people

Dictators

nobody wants. The French refused him an entry visa when he tried to move to his beloved Paris, and he ended up selling tropical swim-wear on the Ivory Coast. In 1983, he managed to obtain entry to France, and took a villa outside Paris. Miraculously, he ended up flat broke, and suffered the indignity of having his water, telephone and electricity cut off. His three children were arrested for shoplifting and he was unable to bail them out. In 1986, he drifted back to Bangui, where, in his absence he had been sentenced to death. This was commuted to life in solitary confinement. He was released in 1993, as part of a general amnesty for all prisoners called by outgoing President Andre Kolingba. Bokassa returned to his family village and his seventeen wives and fifty children. The only state leader ever to be tried for cannibalism died of a heart attack in 1996.

Chapter Eight

Adolf Hitler: The Revenge of a Failed Artist

Night, inside the Bunker, April 1945. The clocks say that day is approaching, but here, deep underground among the suffocating labyrinth of concrete corridors and in the stale offices and conference rooms, the only light is that cast by the sallow coloured bulbs hanging from the ceilings. These tremble and sway gently, registering the fact that above, high-explosive shells are pouring down on what remains of Berlin. In one of the corridors, trying to stay out of public view, an orderly and another soldier with flashes on his collar, indicating his membership of the SS, are haggling grimly over something in a box tied with delicate ribbon. The SS man is adamant about the value of what he has to sell. The orderly doesn't have the time to argue. Reluctantly, he gives in, only asking that he be allowed to view the merchandise. The soldier opens the lid of the box gingerly, and together they both gawp in astonishment. It is a beauty. In the midst of this apocalypse, someone has made an immaculate, vast Black Forest gateau.

Among the ruins, the light of dawn is obscured by a thick pall of oily smoke; an inextinguishable fire burns the city. On the outskirts, old men and children are waiting to fight the Russians. At their backs stand the remaining ranks of the Waffen SS, urging them on with boots and guns. Russian tanks come clanking across the rubble; behind them, the shadows of men flow swiftly from doorway to doorway. All is horror, confusion and inevitable, hopeless defeat.

Dictators

The inhabitants of the underworld have lost track of time or purpose. In contrast to the inferno above, there is a curious, numb quiet. Some are sleeping, others, in the conference rooms, listen to the panic-stricken reports that indicate the scale of the catastrophe. The typists are still tapping out reams of directives to non-existent armies, reprimands to dead men and execution orders for those who have failed, but this is a charade. There is nothing anyone can do; most have no idea why they are still here. A telephone begins to ring. No-one answers it, and after a while it goes dead forever. A few hours ago, they were issued with cyanide capsules and rehearsed a mass suicide as choreographed by Heinrich Himmler, head of the SS, but they don't want to die. Under their subdued tones, there is a dreadful hysteria. Occasional violent squabbles break out. One or two are visibly snivelling, their noses and eyes streaming. All have appalling migraines, and are suffering from acute claustrophobia. Many are only held together by the stretched, narcotic threads of amphetamines and morphine. The sour air smells of fear and sweat. They want to smoke, but Adolf Hitler has strictly forbidden this. For the last month he has screamed ceaselessly at them, in monologues of hatred up to three hours long. They do have one purpose left, to keep him quiet.

Adolf Hitler has been awake all night and is looking forward to his breakfast at 6, after which he will sleep until late in the day. Sitting in the corner of an upright sofa in his office, he has just finished dictating an eighty-page memorandum, giving his generals precise instructions on how to win the war, whilst simultaneously blaming them for Germany's defeat. On his lap is a golden labrador puppy, which he is rhythmically stroking and occasionally whispering endearments to. His hair is lank and his pebbly eyes dull, and between the corners of his mouth and his chin there is a drying beard of spittle.

The hand he is stroking the dog with has a spasmodic tremor. Every so often his left leg picks up this twitch and begins to shake. He struggles to contain this by wrapping his foot tightly round the leg of the sofa. At these times, his body shrinks and goes tense with furious concentration. The memorandum is utterly incoherent.

The exhausted young secretary, who has finished taking dictation, rises and makes for the door. As she opens it Hitler indicates the clock, which now reads 6 in the morning. "Chocolate," he says, appealing with a smile radiating self-pity. It is pleading, greedy and childish, the petulant ghost of his charm. Outside the door, she nearly crashes into the triumphant orderly, who is carrying a tray in to the Führer; on it is hot chocolate and a plate piled high with thick slabs of Black Forest gateau smothered under cream and cherries. The procurement of this under the current circumstances is nothing short of miraculous. Impending destruction has vastly increased Hitler's consumption of sickly pastries.

Hitler tries to stand, but there is something uncertain about his balance, and frantically clutching the dog, he collapses back onto the sofa. "Just two pieces," he lies, in response to the orderly's enquiry as to how much cake the Führer would like, "But leave the tray." And then he adds, excusing his appetite, "I didn't eat much supper last night." The orderly fusses ingratiatingly about his health and hands him the heavy plate. "Ah!" Hitler exclaims in anticipation, addressing the dog, "my darling little Wolf. Can you understand people who do not crave sweets? Art requires nourishment as well as fanaticism." Then he picks up a wedge of gateau and, feigning delicacy for a moment, hesitates, before suddenly pelicaning it. Cream, crumbs of chocolate and a glacé cherry fall onto his revolting, soup-stained suit. He rubs them in and licks more goo off his moustache, absorbed, pausing with pleasure before the next mouthful. Outside, in fields, cities and concentration camps, lie the bodies of fifty million dead.

Adolf Hitler was born on 20 April 1889 in Braunau, Austria, then a part of the vast Austro-Hungarian Empire which was to fall apart in World War I. His father Alois was a customs official, a noted drunkard and rapacious lecher, who married Adolf Hitler's mother, his own second cousin, when he was old enough to be her father. It was his third wedding. He had driven his first wife away when he took up with her maid, who had died within a few years. Klara, young and pretty, had been sent into his care when only sixteen, and he had been violating her for some years. She was already pregnant when they married, though the son that was born died within a few days. Hitler was the fourth of five children of this unhappy union, but only he and a half-witted sister Paula survived infancy. His half-sister, Angela Raubal, had a child, Geli Raubal, who was to be one of the strange loves of his life.

Alois was violent towards both the children and his wife. His death when Adolf was fourteen liberated his mother, who set about spoiling her darling son rotten. Adolf was not an unintelligent pupil at school, but was described as arrogant, argumentative, evasive, sly and above all, lazy. He had a tendency for self-dramatization and assumed the position of misunderstood and persecuted outcast from an early age. He failed to gain a school-leaving certificate, dropping out through illness, and his favourite pastimes were playing war-games and reading endless adventure stories about the North American Indians.

After leaving school, Hitler spent two crucial years in Linz between the ages of sixteen and eighteen. He had decided his vocation was art and his intention was to enter the Vienna Academy of Arts, but he repeatedly put off taking the entrance examination, preferring to fantasize about the extent of his undiscovered talent rather than put it to the test.

Supported by his indulgent mother, he posed around Linz, growing extremely dandified, sketching and painting and drawing up grandiose designs for the complete reconstruction of the city. He dressed like an elegant, wealthy student, and was thrilled to be mistaken for the genuine article. In his conceit he was unsure upon which branch of art to bestow the prodigious gifts he credited himself as possessing. Literature, architecture, music and painting all attracted him; to his dying day, Hitler was vexed by the thought of his neglected talent, exclaiming, "What an artist dies with me!"

In Vienna, Hitler displayed an avid interest in sex without ever having a girlfriend. It is during this period that some theorists maintain that Hitler contracted syphilis from a Jewish prostitute. Quite apart from the final madness this would bring, it would explain his inability to have a normal sex life, and his reliance on a series of extreme perversions to obtain sexual gratification. It was a team of American psychologists, compiling a wartime, mental profile of the "Führer" who concluded that, as consequence of his early experiences, which may have included syphilis, he required young women to urinate and defecate upon him, a fact that was supported by several sadly unidentified partners and his niece Geli Raubal. Certainly, he had developed an obsession with disease, dirt and putrefaction, and the term "shithead" remained one of his favourite and most frequent epithets.

Probably the only syphilitic disease he picked up during these years was his anti-Semitism, his pathological hatred of all things Jewish. No matter how he sought to rationalize this, it remained an irrational, infantile obsession. Just as his laziness was excused by calling himself an "artist", so his failures were explained as the work of the Jews. At the time of his stint in Vienna, it was a city with a large and prosperous Jewish population, who dominated artistic and cultural life. Jealousy of their material or intellectual accomplishments was common. Anti-Semitic pamphlets were cheap and plentiful, and they took pride of place on his shelf, next to his collections of pornography, mythology and that other favourite subject of the idle and envious mind, the occult.

To compound Hitler's self-imposed isolation, his mother died of cancer. Much has been made of the fact that the doctor who could not save her life was Jewish, which Hitler was later fond of pointing out. He was stricken by her death. During the period of her treatment, Hitler authorized the use of painful and futile chemical treatments, saying that "sometimes one must use a poison to drive out a greater poison". The same chlorine-based chemicals were later used to murder millions of Jews in the concentration camps.

Hitler tried again to gain entrance into the Vienna Academy of the Arts, and this time was refused permission to take the examination. At the end of 1908, consumed with self-pity, he disappeared from his lodgings, and without telling anyone of his whereabouts, vanished into the underbelly of Vienna.

Hitler claimed that during the following years he experienced hardship, poverty, unemployment; in short, real life. But he initially still had a good supply of money from private sources and added to this a small but useful income from the sale of dull postcards and sketches of Vienna. He also claimed that he read voraciously, when he merely continued his anti-Semitic "studies".

In 1909, Hitler hit rock bottom, ending up on the streets, hungry and homeless, surviving on handouts of soup and living in a shelter for the destitute. His pretensions to be an artist were now blown away; the spoiled and snobbish young man was now a tramp. From 1910–13 he found a place in a charitable Home for Men. Hitler became one of the established residents in the Home. Without ever forming any close relationships, it gave him an easy forum in which to begin lecturing a captive audience in the reading-room. He did not discuss, he spouted; he had no time for democracy, despising the debates of parliamentary institutions. He scraped a living selling postcards of Vienna copied from photographs.

In 1913, Hitler moved to Munich in the German heartland of Bavaria. He told friends that he intended to enter the Munich Art Academy. He did nothing about this, but fell in love with the city: "A German city! So different from Vienna, that Babylon of races!" He styled himself "painter and writer" and became even more isolated, speaking to no-one apart from the family he lodged with and those he quarrelled with in cafés. Unfortunately, he had forgotten, or avoided, registering for military service in Vienna, and was arrested in Munich. He wrote a desperate, pitiable plea for mercy to the authorities, on the basis of his poverty and ignorance of the law. He was excused both his misdemeanour and, after examination, military service on the grounds of "physical weakness".

Adolf Hitler: The Revenge of a Failed Artist

A year later, the Great War erupted, and Germany and Austria declared war on Russia and Serbia. Internal differences and unrest were forgotten; national unity broke out along with an ecstatic sense of patriotism. The German Kaiser declared everyone to be "German brothers", and to millions of them the war signalled an end to everyday monotony and a clear, simple direction in their lives; to fight. To Hitler, rescued from his aimless existence, the sense of purpose was a blessing: "For me these hours came as a deliverance . . . I sank down on my knees to thank Heaven for the favour of having been permitted to live in such a time."

He volunteered for the army, and to his delight was accepted. After a couple of months training he was sent to the front as a regimental runner. This position suited him ideally; it was with difficulty that he was persuaded to take leave. It was a lonely, dangerous job conveying messages between regiments, and he remained aloof from his fellow soldiers who quickly lost their enthusiasm for the war, for which he furiously and persistently accused them of being traitors. He, of course, was the super-patriot, thrilled to be involved in what he perceived as a racial conflict. He was living out his heroic, mythological fantasies, which nourished his courage.

Without exception, other soldiers and officers found him dreary and odd, and although his devotion to duty resulted in decoration (he was awarded the Iron Cross), he was never promoted beyond the rank of corporal. He never showed any discomfort with the horrors and destruction of the trenches. On the contrary, he enjoyed it all, recounting his experiences with relish. He regarded this complete lack of compassion as proof of his manhood. "War", he would say, in a pronouncement reeking of Wagnerian gloom, "is for a man what childbirth is for a woman"; he could not distinguish between the values of life and death.

Hitler was lying in hospital, suffering from the after-effect of a gas attack, when news came of the Armistice, by which Germany surrendered. By the treaty of Versailles, Germany was required to make vast payments to its former enemies in compensation. In addition, thirteen per cent of its territory was taken away, and it was disarmed. For Hitler, and other right-wing nationalists, it was a moment of complete humiliation; those who signed the treaty were regarded as traitors.

Hitler, failed school-pupil, failed artist, social misfit, successful soldier on the losing side and leader-in-waiting, first went to a meeting of the German Workers' Party on 12 September 1919. He was disappointed with the Workers' Party at his first encounter, but went again with the encouragement of the founder, who had been impressed by Hitler's fluency in a tirade he had launched at the meeting. Hitler, after some hesitation, joined the Party as member responsible for recruitment and propaganda. A career in politics had to start somewhere; none of the big parties would offer an opportunity to a nobody. On 16 October 1919, he made his first public speech, and a great career as an actor was launched. "I talked for thirty minutes, and what I had always felt deep down in my heart was . . . was here proved true; I could make a good speech."

Hitler soon had the name of the party changed to the "National Socialist German Workers' Party" – the Nazis – and by 1921 he had become its "Führer".

Hitler's skill as an orator and actor grew to a peak at the huge, staged rallies of the 1930s, when there was a distinctly sexual relationship between him and his massed audiences. His technique had a particular effect on women, who not infrequently experienced orgasm listening to his rhetoric. It was said that "Hitler!" was a popular exclamation for German house-wives to utter at the moment of ecstasy. Homosexual listeners experienced a similar excitement. His attitude to the crowd was not to persuade, but appeal to their feelings, to do what God refused to – liberate them from reason and responsibility.

Beneath the barely coherent language of his speeches lurked a sado-masochistic relationship, in which he alternately beat and flattered the crowd, controlling the relationship as he whipped it towards a peak of ecstatic emotional excitement. He gained as

Adolf Hitler: The Revenge of a Failed Artist

> Hitler was an animated, passionate speech maker, who appealed to the emotions of his audience rather than their reason, and fed off their excitement, fears and hopes. It was to prove a vital discovery.

much from this as the crowds, and, like a lover, would thank them after the climax. This was the closest human relationship he possessed. As Otto Strasser, one of the original Nazis who later deserted Hitler, said: "Hitler responds to the vibrations of the human heart with the delicacy of a seismograph or perhaps of a wireless set . . . enabling him to act as a loudspeaker proclaiming the most secret desires, the least admissible instincts, the suffering and personal grievances of a whole nation . . . he sniffs the air . . . he gropes . . . he feels his way . . . senses the atmosphere. Suddenly he bursts forth. His words go like an arrow to their target . . . telling it what it most wants to hear . . ."

When his performance was combined with the vast stage spectacles of the Nuremberg rallies, the Germans willingly fell under his spell, and freely put themselves in the hands of the failed artist and former tramp from Braunau. In spite of his passion, he never lost sight of his objectives in a speech; the whole experience remained remarkably calculating. He would practise his facial expressions in the mirror for hours, and take a long time to warm up, to sense the mood of his audience, before moving into gear, with a series of simple, repeated statements and questions to which the audience could only answer "yes" or "no". There were no complexities to be found in his speeches and he wanted no thought from an audience. A speech lasted two or more hours. Leaving them, in a style that Hollywood would admire, with an up-beat, optimistic ending, they always wanted more. In the crucial elections of the 1930s, he would make several speeches a night, dashing around the country by aeroplane.

Dictators

To back up propaganda was violence. The Nazis formed a paramilitary wing called the SA, or "Brownshirts". These thugs, made up of disillusioned ex-soldiers, carried out whatever intimidation and brutality was necessary against political rivals, particularly the Communists. The head of the SA was Ernst Rohm, a fat ex-soldier, who had a team of pimps scouring the school-yards of Munich to keep him supplied with the boys that were his pleasure. Hitler was hanging around with an unsavoury crew in those Munich days; a collection of misfits, sexual bandits, seedy ex-convicts, decadent aristocrats and occult weirdos. A less qualified collection of hopeful ministers was never seen.

The conditions were ideal for the Nazis. In the wake of the Great War, Germany was a humiliated, poor, and turbulent country. There was an awful vacuum where there should have been leadership; the Kaiser had been forced to abdicate, and Germany had highly unstable governments, cobbled together from endlessly quarrelling coalitions of parties, which toppled monthly. Depression and astonishing inflation added to the chaos. In November 1923, a thousand billion marks had the same spending power as one solitary mark had in 1914. The final crippling blow were the immense sums Germany still had to pay in compensation to her wartime enemies. The country was a black hole, in which any monster might arise. In Italy too the fascists were in the ascendancy.

Hitler's new party, devoid of policies which might confuse the voters, and with simple explanations for Germany's ills, was successful enough for him to attempt to mount a violent takeover of the State of Bavaria in November 1923. Starting with a meeting at a beer cellar in Munich, the Nazis planned to eventually march on Berlin itself. Hitler was uneasy about the whole event, but was persuaded that there would be support from the army and police. The plan was a fiasco, in which he was notably distinguished by his lack of heroism. The Bavarian Police opened fire, killing sixteen, and Hitler ended up in prison.

Hitler opening the 1934 Nuremberg rally, where he was welcomed by nearly a million Nazis. *Popperfoto*

Dictators

He was sentenced to five years, but only served nine months. During this time he wrote *Mein Kampf* with its 164,000 grammatical and syntactical mistakes, enjoyed considerable comfort and received as many visitors as he pleased. When he came out, he was a hero.

Hitler was the Nazis' greatest asset; as far as he was concerned, he was the Party. Hitler, so long an outcast, had now become a celebrity. His company was sought at the houses of the rich and famous. He dined with industrialists, and spent weekends at the home of Winifred Wagner, granddaughter of his idol the composer; his pride and pleasure knew no bounds. He remained lazy, having little time for the day-to-day running of affairs. Being a genius, he needed time to think, and was frequently in retreat at his country hideaway at Berchtesgaden.

Nevertheless, he had a very clear idea of what he wanted. After the failure of the attempt to seize power by use of force, he was determined that he should ascend the throne legally. It is common for dictators to desire their terror to be sanctioned by law; they are forever holding elections at which they are the only candidate. He drove the Nazi Party on over ten years and countless disappointments. By 1932, it was the largest single Party, with over fourteen million votes but could not win an outright majority over the ruling conservative and nationalist coalition. What Hitler could do was force election after election to continually destabilize the authorities, to gnaw away at their support until they were at last forced to do a deal with him, and invite him to join the coalition.

Of the seven women known to have had relationships of some sort with Hitler, no less than six committed or attempted to commit suicide. Suicide, we are told, is often a reaction induced by shame in the wake of enforced sexual deviancy. Some of these deaths are deeply suspicious giving the impression that women who came to know Hitler's intimate habits rather too well were disposed of if they threatened to reveal them. One of the more dramatic is the death of Renate Mueller, a well-known film actress, whom Hitler invited back to his quarters one evening. She confided in tears to her director that after graphically describing the process of Gestapo torture to her, Hitler, who had become increasingly animated, fell on the floor in front of her and begged to be beaten. Pleading that he was unworthy, he demanded that she kick him. The scene became unbearable, and she finally gave in to his wishes. The more she kicked him, the more excited he became. Shortly after relating this, she mysteriously flew out of the window of a Berlin hotel. This was in 1937, with the Nazis firmly in power and her death was ruled a suicide.

Before this there was Geli Raubal, daughter of his half-sister, Angela. After Hitler's holiday in prison, he summoned Angela and her daughter to work as his housekeepers. Geli, in her late teens had become something of a beauty. Hitler's interest went well beyond that of a friendly uncle. She was blonde and youthful, the Nazis' dream of an Aryan maiden. Straight out of Wagner, she went straight to Hitler's heart.

The incestuous overtones made it more appealing. Before long, the seventeen-year-old had been set up in a Munich apartment, and was being escorted around town by "Uncle Alf". He even paid for her singing lessons with the best available teachers to complete the fantasy by turning her into a Wagnerian opera singer. Hitler was infatuated, which did not go unnoticed by those around him. Complaints were made that Hitler was "excessively diverted from his political duties by the constant company of his niece".

In 1929, Hitler bought a luxurious apartment in Munich, exiled Geli's mother to his weekend house, and moved Geli in with him. They had separate bedrooms, but on the same floor. Hitler was extremely possessive about her, and having initially enjoyed the power and celebrity that was hers through her relationship with the rising star of German politics, she was increasingly cooped in and suffocated by Hitler's jealousy. She was frightened of what she had found inside him.

She had been plotting to escape for several months when, on 18 September 1931, she died. It was another "suicide". Geli shot herself in the chest after an argument with Hitler. The true circumstances surrounding her death are a continuing controversy. It is thought that she was murdered, either on Hitler's orders, or by Nazis who feared her influence on Hitler. Certainly her death was rapidly covered up and the body hastily buried with the co-operation of the right-wing authorities.

Fritz Gerlich, a journalist who claimed to have conclusive evidence of Hitler's involvement with her murder, was killed before he could print his evidence. All his documents were burned and his secret died with him, but before her death, Geli had confided to Strasser the nature of Hitler's sexual requirements – that she was obliged to urinate on him. Revelations of this sort would have been most damaging to his career.

By this time, he was already having an affair with Eva Braun, which continued until their mutual suicide in 1945. Being Hitler's girlfriend was no fun. He never called, showed her little or no affection, never told her his whereabouts and flirted incessantly with other women, who found this reptile quite charming and fascinating, though physically he was not impressive, being short and flabby with spindly limbs and rotting teeth. He preferred women who were petite and blonde like his mother. He might flatter the others, but he knew what he liked: "A woman must be a cute, cuddly, naive little thing – tender, sweet and stupid . . ."

Against a background of growing racial violence and outright murder engineered by his own Brownshirts, Hitler broke into the Government in 1933 as part of a coalition, personally taking the position of Chancellor. The politicians who had done deals with the Nazis in order to keep a measure of power for their own parties were now gobbled up. They had assumed that he would simply shoot the Communists, which showed how little they understood Hitler. Von Papen, the Vice-Chancellor, had boasted that Hitler was not to be taken seriously. "No danger at all," he said. "We've hired him for our act." Overseas, few could take Hitler seriously on a personal level and failed to see how the Germans could do so on a national scale. The British firmly believed the Nazis had peaked and no longer presented a threat.

A stage-managed fire at the seat of Government allowed Hitler to declare a state of emergency. Under threat of using his legal powers to dissolve the Government and throw the country in chaos once more, he obtained an Enabling Act which gave him dictatorial powers and banned all other political parties. Unbelievably, still without a practical policy to their name, the Nazis had triumphed. The failed artist was about to have his revenge.

The Nazi manifesto had been simple. Faced with a country in a severe economic crisis, they promised to solve everything by restoring German pride. This meant tearing up the Treaty of Versailles. They would refuse to pay compensation; they would rearm; they would reclaim Germany's lost lands and extend these to provide "Lebensraum" or living room for the great German race, and they would solve the Jewish problem, which naturally included the Communists. In other words, Hitler's policy was to wage war and spill blood.

Whilst his nation geared up for war, Hitler began to suffer physical problems to accompany his mental sickness. He had long been principally vegetarian because of bowel problems. After Geli's death he never touched meat again, complaining that it was like eating corpses. The bowel problems of abdominal pains, constipation and vast flatulence increased. He began to see a quack doctor, Theo Morrel, who became his constant companion. By the end of the war, Hitler was taking up to thirty drugs and vitamin compounds for his real and imagined complaints.

Morrel's favourite treatment, which Hitler took huge quantities of, was called "Mutaflor". In keeping with his paranoid theories about the Jews, Hitler saw himself being persecuted by "noxious bacteria" which had "invaded" his colon. Mutaflor, claimed Morrel, would replace the evil bacteria with a pure Aryan strain cultured from the faeces of "a Bulgarian peasant of the most vigorous stock".

Morrel also started giving Hitler painkilling injections for his bowel pains. These contained amphetamines, and it is medically thought that Hitler became addicted to the drugs, which perked him up.

Driven by a policy of huge deficit spending, Germany rearmed, flaunting the Versailles treaty, building the autobahns that would carry its troops to war. By 1938, Germany faced something of a financial crisis. There was nothing left in the kitty. The war which Hitler planned had to begin.

First to go was Austria, which was annexed as part of Germany without a fight. Hitler could now claim that he was German by birth; the Rhineland, under French occupation since the end of the Great War, had already been infiltrated by his soldiers. Czechoslovakia and then Poland were attacked under the pretext that he was acting to protect German minorities within them. He treated Czechoslovakia like cake, claiming he only wanted a little piece of it, then wolfing the whole country. He called it a "ridiculous state", rightfully German property. Chamberlain, the British Prime Minister, flew to meet him, and came back clutching a worthless agreement to "peace in our time". Hitler signed a non-aggression treaty with Stalin, in which they agreed to help themselves to Poland, and on 31 August 1939, the Germans launched a Blitzkrieg which swept the million strong but antiquated Polish army away within hours.

There was no way back. In Hitler's words: "I go the way that providence guides me, with the assurance of a sleepwalker."

Britain and France declared war. After twenty-nine postponements, the invasion of France took place in Spring 1940. It was a daring and completely successful plan created by General Erich von Marsten. So rapidly did the Germans advance that Hitler lost his nerve several times, afraid that his tanks were too far ahead of the rest of his army. The troops were equally matched on both sides, but the Germans had an overwhelming superiority in terms of hardware. The screaming dive-bombers, fitted with Wagnerian sirens on Hitler's orders, smashed a path for the massive panzer tank divisions. After them poured the troops.

Adolf Hitler: The Revenge of a Failed Artist

Within six weeks they had the French army in tatters and the British on the beach at Dunkirk. It was here that Hitler decided to halt the advance, frightened by his success. Goering promised that the air force would finish off the British troops. They failed, and the British managed the remarkable evacuation.

Hitler was now master of greater Europe. His forces were in Norway, Africa and Greece. Italy was an ally, and Spain neutral but friendly. He was now sure of his military genius, took less advice and shouted more. His quarelling generals began to simply agree with him. The planned invasion of England was to be preceded by massive air strikes against military and civilian targets. On "Eagle Day", 13 August 1940, Goering's air force began to bomb Britain. By 17 September, the raids had stopped in the face of huge losses. On one day, seventy-one aircraft were downed. Hitler could not afford to sustain these losses indefinitely. Germany had a limited supply of oil and raw materials. To build the Third Reich they would have to conquer Russia.

Stalin, although he knew that war with Germany was inevitable, was buying time, and picking up any territorial scraps that Hitler overlooked. Hitler had plans for Russia, when he had subjugated the inferior Slavs to their correct position as slaves of the German master-race: "This Russian desert . . . we shall populate it. We'll take away its character of an Asiatic steppe, we'll Europeanize it. With this object in mind we have undertaken the construction of roads. Studded along their whole length will be German towns and around these towns our colonists will settle . . ."

Everything outside Germany was a wasteland inhabited by sub-humans to be enslaved, part turned into one enormous, Nazi holiday camp, the remainder reserved for slave-labour and extermination. The "Final Solution" began in 1941. Poland was turned into an abattoir. Of the eighteen million victims of Nazi brutality in Europe, eleven million died on Polish soil. Of that eleven million, five million were Jews. The names of these places in which, without compassion, young and old of both sexes, were systematically gassed, shot, tortured, starved and worked to death with complete indifference on the part of their German captors will never be forgotten; Dachau, Buchenwald, Belzec, Chelmno, Treblinka, Mauthausen and the model of hell-on-earth, the heart of the Third Reich, the inside of Hitler's head and the summit of his art, Auschwitz.

In June 1941, operation "Barbarossa", the invasion of Russia, began. Behind the three separate armies that smashed their way into Russia went the "Einsatzgruppen", the extermination squads sent to liquidate the "Jewish-Bolshevik ruling class". Over 300,000 civilians were killed in the first six months. Of the 5,700,000 Russian prisoners taken, barely one million survived the war. Instead of casting themselves as an army come to liberate the Russians from the repression of the Stalinist regime, they continued their policy of racist genocide, thus motivating the Russians to fight tooth and nail.

In Africa, Rommel began his campaign victoriously. For a time, it looked as if the Nazis might, unbelievably, prevail.

A year later, in November 1942, the tide turned. Although the war would go on for another two and a half years, the Germans could no longer emerge victorious. In Africa, Rommel was defeated at El Alamein. America had joined the war. The Allies were bombing Germany. And crucially, in Russia, the Germans came to a grinding halt in the carnage of the Eastern Front.

Hitler began increasingly to isolate himself, rarely emerging from his rural hideaway, the "Wolf's Lair", a depressing complex in the midst of a thick and gloomy forest in Prussia. He aged rapidly, and his consumption of drugs rocketed. He refused to read reports about the military situation and bomb damage to Germany, like a petulant actor who will not read the bad reviews. He ate with his secretaries who were forbidden to mention the war. After 1943, he made only two speeches.

Rather than seek practical ways to increase Germany's military hopes, Hitler looked for miracle weapons to bring him victory. This was a consequence of his love of mythology; he believed in magic more than people and science only when it supported his preconceptions; above all, like most dabblers in the occult, he wanted instant results. It is due to his impatience that he gave little serious attention to the Atomic bomb; he preferred to send his VI and V2 rockets over the English Channel. Though they killed nearly 10,000 civilians, they were hopelessly inaccurate and militarily insignificant. He had no interest in defensive weapons as the possibility of retreat and defeat had not occurred to him. He threw his armies forwards into hopeless battle and inglorious death. In 1943, the Allies declared that they would not seek a peace settlement; they would accept only "unconditional surrender".

In June 1944, the Allies landed in France. Rommel, who was in charge of coastal defences, was on his way to see Hitler when the news broke, Hitler was asleep, and no-one dared disturb him. By the time he woke up in the afternoon and ordered, with a typical lack of realism, that "the enemy must be annihilated at the bridgehead by the evening of 6 June", the Allies were well ensconced. Within ten days, 600,000 troops were ashore. By the end of a month, nearly a million. Hitler could not accept it. He was convinced that the Allies could not hold together, that their alliance would collapse, that the British would fight the Russians, that his miracle weapons would destroy their spirit. In the East, the Russians expelled the Germans from their territory. They were only four hundred miles from Berlin.

There were heroes inside the Church, and the army, who understood the nature of the evil the Nazis had created, and others who now realized the suicide that Hitler intended for Germany. They realized Hitler had to die. Henning von Tresckow, one of a small number of high-ranking army officers who were involved with the bomb-plot to kill Hitler that Summer, wrote to his fellow conspirator Klaus von Stauffenberg: "The assassination must be attempted at all costs . . . Even should it fail . . . we must prove to the world and to future generations that the men of the German Resistance dared to take this step and hazard their lives upon it . . ."

Many of these men were highly decorated, gallant and

intelligent soldiers from old German families. Von Stauffenberg, crippled and blind in one eye with war-wounds, planted a brief-case with a bomb in it under a table in the conference room on 20 July. They had made earlier attempts on his life, but the bombs had refused to go off. After his death, they planned to use the army to take Berlin and sweep the Nazis away. The bomb did explode, but by a freak Hitler survived.

In the resulting purge, the principal conspirators, who had gathered together in expectation of Hitler's death, were shot or committed suicide. Planned rebellions by the army in Germany and France stuttered and faltered when they heard Hitler was alive. Himmler and the Gestapo went to work. Field Marshal von Witzleben, Generals Hoepner, von Hase and Stieff, together with four others were hanged by piano wires from meat-hooks, a means of death by slow throttling which is prolonged and agonizing. Hitler had a film made of the execution, and watched and re-watched it with delight. The men, who had been tortured for days, showed considerable dignity.

The failure of the bomb plot rejuvenated the will of the deranged Führer. Now he was convinced Heaven had spared him. It also reassured him that all the defeats he had suffered were due entirely to treachery on the part of his generals. For the little that remained of his life, he excluded from power anyone he did not feel was personally loyal to him. Goebbels, Himmler and Bormann, all fanatical Nazis, wielded the power. Each strove to establish a personal empire amidst the ruins.

On 25 August, Paris was liberated. On 11 September, an American patrol crossed the German frontier. The war had come home to Hitler, five years after his assault on Poland.

He moved into the Bunker permanently. From above ground, it looked like an Egyptian tomb. Its concrete walls, sixteen feet thick, further insulated Hitler from the outside world. In December, the Germans launched a desperate bid to break the Allied lines in the Ardennes with the object of taking Antwerp. It was Hitler's last encore, and an entirely futile military gesture, which sacrificed the last of the German reserves. The offensive

26 April 1945. The Bunker is shaking as the Chancellery above is shelled and collapses. The Russians are now only a mile away. Hitler cannot understand why nothing has been done to launch a counter-attack. He is hysterical with rage; all who hear him are shaken and exhausted; "I expect the relief of Berlin! Where is Heinrici's army? Where is Wenck's army? I expect them!"

Eva Braun and Goebbels have announced their intention of seeking death among the ruins with him. They too have moved into the Bunker. In the words of Hitler's architect, Speer, who secretly calls the Bunker the "Isle of the Departed", so far away from life are its inhabitants: ". . . he had reached the last station of his flight from reality, a reality which he had refused to acknowledge since youth."

was opposed by most of the surviving army officers, whom Hitler shouted down. This was the "Battle of the Bulge". After an initial success, which Hitler trumpeted as the greatest victory of the war, they suffered terrible losses – 100,000 men, 600 tanks, 1,600 aircraft – and were compelled to withdraw. A month after the attack, they were once again in full retreat. People began to hide from Hitler, who was seeking consolation in a vast, illuminated model of the rebuilding he planned for his home town of Linz. He was returning in his mind to those far-off days when, posing as a student, he had sketched and dreamed of the great, though undefined, destiny that lay in store for him.

As his own suicide drew nearer, he ordered a scorched-earth policy, and the destruction of anything which might be used to rebuild Germany after the war: "If the war is lost, the people will be lost also . . . In any case only those who are inferior will remain after this struggle . . ."

Dictators

He showed no concern for the fate of his people; he took no responsibility for the defeat. He thought only of himself.

Hitler will not consider surrender. His speech has become an invariable string of meaningless phrases: "no retreat; only with permission; accepting the risk; concentrated bold and determined attack; fanatical will". Even the most faithful rats are baling out. Himmler is off trying to do a deal with the Allies. Goering has already tried. Neither will succeed. When Hitler finds out they too have betrayed him, he orders their arrest and shoots those connected with them. Speer is refusing to follow his orders to blow up the world. His armies are rushing west to surrender to the British and Americans; anything to avoid the Russians. When not shouting, he dribbles and talks incessantly about his two Golden Labradors, Blondi, and the little puppy, Wolf. He will not let anybody touch Wolf. He has a stock of dog stories and repeats them over and over again. He eats only vegetable soup, cake and drugs.

A few insufferable days later, on the evening of the 29th, with the enemy only streets away, he marries Eva Braun. Since she has volunteered to die with him, he has been affectionate with her. They drink champagne, and talk about the old days. Hitler, armed with cake, retires to dictate his Last Political Will and Testament. In this he again disclaims all responsibility for all that has happened, and claims that: "I myself, as founder and creator of the movement have preferred death to cowardly abdication or even capitulation."

Hitler is finally going to kill himself. He has washed his hands of those he has led to their destruction, in whom he invoked the power of old myths to encourage acts of unspeakable evil, to enact his fantasies for him.

It is now the afternoon of the 30th. Outside the door of Hitler's suite, they are tense, waiting for the moment when this nightmare will end. Hitler and his wife have said their goodbyes. Someone murmurs the news that Mussolini has been caught and shot by Italian partisans, his body hung up to public ridicule in Milan. Hitler's chauffeur thinks momentarily about the two hundred litres of petrol he has acquired on Hitler's orders. He wonders if it will be enough to obliterate the bodies. Will they be safe, burning them above, while the shells come raining down?

At last, a shot. After a brief struggle with the door, they enter. At either end of an upright sofa are Mr and Mrs Adolf Hitler. He has shot himself in the temple, she is dead from poison. The spell begins to drop from the followers immediately. There is a strange lifting, a sense of release. Adolf Hitler is dead. In a few days Germany will surrender. But the world, thank God, has not been destroyed by the failed artist from Braunau.

Chapter Nine

Vlad Dracul:
The Impaler Strikes Back

The rehabilitation of dead dictators by their successors in tyranny is common; the new always looks to the old to justify itself. If the image of the old is grubby, the official historians are sent to clean it up.

Nicolae Ceaucescu, the late, despised President of Rumania, often drew comparison with the legendary Rumanian tyrant, Vlad Dracul or Dracula, better known as Vlad the Impaler, who was three times king of Wallachia between 1448 and 1476. Wallachia is one of the three main provinces of modern Rumania, and is considered to be the symbolic heartland of the country. As his name suggests, Vlad was well-known for punishing his enemies by impaling them, which earned him a fearsome reputation even in an age where being burned alive was the equivalent of receiving a parking-fine. Bram Stoker, whose novel *Dracula* was much inspired by Rumanian folk-tales, gave Vlad's other name to his blood-sucking Count Dracula, who was proud to claim descent from the ferocious Wallachian Prince. The Americans felt that *Dracula* was such a good representation of the Communist menace that they made the novel recommended reading for their troops. It was not an image that Ceaucescu enjoyed, and his historians were unleashed in an attempt to prove that Vlad had been slandered, that he should be remembered as a great patriot, who never kebabbed a man without good reason.

Impaling is a very old form of execution. It is described by the Greeks, and was much practised by the ancient Turkish regimes. It was the Turks who first gave Vlad the title of "Kazakli", meaning Impaler, which in Rumanian is "Tepes". In Vlad's time, impalement was also practised in Transylvania, then part of neighbouring Hungary.

It was not a short, swift death. The stakes on which people were impaled were carefully rounded at the end and bathed in oil, so that the entrails of the victims should not be pierced by a wound too immediately fatal. The legs of the victim were stretched apart by horses and attendants held the stake steady while the body was dragged onto it. The stake was then hoisted upright, and the victim was slowly impaled by the force of their own weight. Not everybody was impaled from the buttocks upwards, but sometimes through the heart, stomach and chest. It is estimated that Vlad disposed of over 100,000 unwanted opponents in this manner over a six-year period. There are many German woodcuts from the period showing graphic representations of these atrocities. A bishop visiting the court of Matthias Corvinus, King of neighbouring Hungary at the time was told: "That 40,000 men and women of the opposite faction had been put to death shortly beforehand upon Vlad Tepes' order subject to the most devilish torments. He killed some by breaking them under the wheels of carts; others stripped of their clothes were skinned alive up to their entrails; others placed upon stakes, or roasted upon red-hot coals placed under them; others punctured with stakes piercing their head, their breast, their buttocks, and the middle of their entrails with the stake emerging from their mouths; and in order that no form of cruelty shall be missing he stuck stakes in both the mothers' breasts and thrust their babies unto them. Finally he killed them in various ferocious ways, torturing them with many kinds of instruments such as the atrocious cruelties of the most frightful tyrant could devise . . ."

Even in his own times, the reputation of Vlad Dracul exerted a profound grip on the imagination. The modern Rumanians would attempt to show that these incidents, although they undeniably happened, were exaggerated by the fifteenth-century Germans, who took to writing propaganda pamphlets about Vlad, with titles like "About the bad Tyrant, Dracula", and "About a great tyrant named Dracula". Ceaucescu's historians claimed that Vlad had punished German merchants for their greed, and these had retaliated by blackening the name of the "Defender of the Christian World".

The date of Vlad the Impaler's birth is uncertain. He was probably born and brought up in Sighishoara, a Transylvanian town. Confusingly, his father, Vlad II, also had the title of Dracul. This translates as "Devil", which may be in reference to his cruelty, but may also have something to do with his coat of arms given to him by the Hungarian ruler, Sigismund. This featured a dragon, from which "Dracul" can be traced. Hence, Dracula means son of the devil, or dragon. Some Rumanians tried to argue that the title "devil" shows affection, as in "he's a devil of a fellow", but this seems somewhat hopeful, although the Turks definitely did admire the Impaler's handiwork. One Rumanian historian even advanced the argument that Dracul is derived from "Drago", meaning "dear one". Ho ho.

At the time of Vlad Dracul's childhood in the first half of the fifteenth century, Wallachia was just emerging as an important strategic province, forming a valuable buffer between Christian Hungary and Moslem Turkey. Whilst realizing the mutual benefit they enjoyed from having such a punch-bag, these two great powers were forever seeking to establish a hold over it, and made sure it was governed by someone loyal to their respective rulers. Vlad II maintained a difficult balancing act between these two, falling off the swing several times. After being dethroned by the Hungarians for allowing the Turks to use Wallachia as a military base to attack them, he was reinstalled by the Turks in 1444. As security for his future conduct, they took his sons Vlad Dracul and Radu The Handsome into Turkey, as hostages. This period in Turkish captivity probably provided Vlad with a unique opportunity to study their applied use of terror. He must also have feared for his life, as meanwhile Vlad Senior had teamed up with the Hungarians and rashly started a Christian Crusade against the Turks, which failed. In the aftermath of defeat, the Christian Allies started quarrelling as to whose fault it was. Vlad lost this battle too, and was killed by the

Hungarians. His eldest son, Mircea, who had stayed with him, was tortured and buried alive. The Hungarians took over Wallachia.

Dracula claimed his inheritance with Turkish help in 1448, but was booted out by the Hungarians a month later, who put a man called Vladislav on the throne. Dracula spent the next eight years worming his way back into favour with the Hungarians, who finally decided in 1456, that they no longer cared for Vladislav, and Dracula got his kingdom back. On 6 September 1456 he took an oath of allegiance to the Hungarian King, and a few days later he pledged obedience to the Turks. It was a tricky situation.

In the following six years, the Impaler struck back, ruling with a ruthlessness and full-blooded commitment to cruelty previously unseen in Europe. Ceaucescu's historians argued that his principal targets were the potentially traitorous and wealthy aristocratic or "Boyar" class, the German merchants and the non-Christian Turks, plus those that he thought to be "idle" or "dishonest", with the result that the people were so terrified, crime, or any form of dissent, was unknown, making Wallachia a paradise for the poor but loyal, hard-working and honest peasant. This is merely justifying Ceaucescu's own extremes. There are folk stories and histories that see Dracula as "just", but his behaviour in them has nothing to do with our idea of justice, and everything to do with inspiring blind obedience through sheer terror. The sixteenth-century historian, Sebastian Munster, wrote:

"It is recalled that Dracula was unimaginably cruel, and just. When the Turkish envoys refused to honour him and take their caps off, because that was their old age custom, he is said to have strengthened their custom by ordering their caps to be fixed with three nails to their heads so that they could never take them off again; and he had numberless Turks impaled while he was feasting amidst them with his friends. Besides, he had all the beggars and idlers, the sick, the poor, the old and the destitute; all the miserable people gathered to a feast and when they had eaten everything up and were dizzy with wine he had the house burnt down to ashes. He was said to have had the feet of Turkish prisoners skinned and rubbed with salt and while they were moaning with pain, goats were admitted to lick their soles and make their suffering greater . . ."

"Just" merely indicates a perverted notion of equality. Vlad displayed considerable imagination in devising suitable grisly punishments to fit the crime. The poor and sick could sleep easily, assured that they would be accorded the same ghastly treatment as the healthy and wealthy.

In one folk story, Dracula comes across a peasant wearing badly fitting clothes, which he takes as a sure sign that the man's wife is lazy. In spite of the man's protestations that he is very happy with his wife, who works too hard to worry about his clothes, Vlad has her impaled and marries the peasant to another woman. She is so terrified of meeting the same fate that she doesn't even stop to eat, and works with her bread on one shoulder and salt on the other, nibbling on the move. In a Russian story, Vlad so hated dishonesty or evil that if anyone so much as told a lie they faced impalement. The legend says he put a gold cup by a remote fountain for the use of travellers, and though it was unguarded, no-one dare steal it. In other folk-tales, Dracula has a fetish for tidiness and a reputation as an impatient master: "Woe to any soldier he saw improperly attired, he rarely escaped with his life . . . he could not tolerate anyone who was slow in his work." The modern Rumanian historians, choosing slyly to present these legends as literal history, saw in them evidence of a man of morality, upright, demanding, severe perhaps, but always with a purpose – to create good, well-behaved citizens; an insidious attempt to justify the Stalinist terror of Ceaucescu by invoking a revamped Dracula as his noble precedent. These old tales show nothing of the sort; they show that so deep was the fear Dracula inspired that he endures in folk stories as a bogeyman used to frighten children into behaving themselves. When adults used to tell children to say their prayers or they would go to Hell, they surely did not mean to suggest that the Devil approved of prayer.

Meanwhile, back in fifteenth-century Wallachia, Vlad set out to exterminate potential opponents and to restrict the trade the Saxon merchants carried out. The towns of Sibiu and Brasov were the scenes of major impalements in 1457–8. He believed he might find his half-brother and rival, Vlad the Monk, at Sibiu, and raided it, impaling and burning women and children. At Brasov, other claimants to the throne were thought to be hiding, besides its being a Saxon stronghold. This old, fortified town is overlooked by St Jacob's Hill, 1,200 feet high. The many he chose to impale here rather than kill immediately must have made an awesome sight, planted in droves up the rocky slopes. It is claimed that up to 30,000 died, though this is certainly exaggerated. The German prints that began to circulate recording this massacre, show him happily sitting amongst this forest, munching on human remains. Understandably, it is from this point that his reputation rapidly declined. A noble who was unable to bear the stench and complained was impaled on an extra large stake with the words: "You live up there, where the smell cannot reach you!"

Dracula was obsessed with eliminating possible pretenders to his throne, and caught up with another, Danciel III, in 1460. Having literally been forced to dig his grave, Danciel was obliged to deliver his own obituary before being decapitated. Only seven of his supporters escaped. The remainder were impaled with their families for company.

At this point in his history we find the story of the Turkish envoys, whose turbans, which they were forbidden by their religion to remove, were nailed to their heads. It has been written that this shows Dracula's sense of dignity; everyone had to take off their hats in his presence, but he was simply spoiling for a fight with the Turks. He should have been paying them 10,000 ducats a year and sending them five hundred boys for their army. Instead of this he put their bills and reminders on the fire and chased any stray envoys out of the country. Those whom he caught were skewered in the usual manner.

Dictators

The old Boyar, or aristocratic class, who might have been a threat to his authority, were exterminated *en masse* in one highly successful evening. He invited them, and their families, to dinner at his castle at Tirgoviste. Surprisingly, they fell for it, and five hundred men, women and children joined the growing plantation of human lollipops outside the city walls. A few, principally young men, were spared in order to work as slave labour on the construction of another castle at Poenar.

Predictably, the Turks wanted to have a word with him. Dracula was evasive. He refused to leave the country for talks on the grounds that he feared a revolt in his absence, a not altogether unlikely scenario. A meeting was arranged in neighbouring Bulgaria. This was still Turkish territory, but at least Dracula was not obliged to travel to Constantinople, a long and dangerous trip. Dracula, however, suspected a trap, and pre-empted any Turkish move by ambushing the Turks' envoy, Hamza Pasha. Then, masquerading as the Turkish party, Dracula's troops entered the Turkish border stronghold of Giurgiu, which they utterly destroyed and set on fire. Dracula beheaded the envoys, and took the captives back to the comfort of Tirgoviste where he added their impaled bodies to his thriving, maggoty collection. Having enraged the Turks, he then courted the Hungarians for support in his escalating dispute, sending the Hungarian King, Matthias Corvinus, a consignment of Turkish delight: two bags full of noses, ears and heads to show he was serious.

Over five hundred years later, Ceaucescu would cast himself as the defender of his country and the true Stalinist faith. He considered it vital that Dracula should appear in the history books as a Christian Crusader, and his campaigns against the Turks were therefore blown up in importance, though they achieved little. Dracula plunged into war for his own reasons and then could not persuade the rest of Europe to join him in what he tried to portray as a Holy Crusade. Perhaps he was just not their cup of tea.

Dracula ravaged the countryside along the Danube to the Black Sea killing, in his own words, an estimated 24,000

Dracula was not a believer in the free market. The German traders were again massacred at the port of Braila. Four hundred Saxon apprentices and older merchants were burned alive and impaled. Most of them were only boys who were there to learn the language. Ceaucescu's historians decided that they were almost certainly "spies". Ceaucescu himself feared the Hungarian and German minorities living in Rumania. It was Hungarians who initiated the revolution against him. When they revolted, he ordered a Dracula-like response, sending gunmen in to mow down the crowds.

"without counting those who we burned in their homes or whose heads we did not take". As his figure was based on the number of heads he took home with him, the estimate is reliable. The Turkish Sultan Mohammed II invaded with a force of 60,000, twice the size of Dracula's army, with the intention of putting the less bloodthirsty Prince Radu on the throne. In spite of bitter fighting and a scorched-earth policy, Dracula was forced to retreat towards Tirgoviste. The Turks followed him. Dracula prepared a suitable spectacle for them.

The country the Turks marched through on their way to Tirgoviste was burned, desolate and unusually quiet. It was an uneasy experience. Just outside the city, they came across a sight that halted them in dismay and horror. In a narrow gulley a mile long were the impaled bodies of 20,000 Turks, Boyars, women and children. In some accounts the amount is even greater, with the forest of pales extending for three kilometres. Crows and vultures had made their nests in the chests of the corpses, which had, to all intents and purposes, become unholy trees. The Sultan was shocked and impressed by this display of torture and carnage, and, it is claimed, admitted that he could not take the land from a man who was capable of doing such things to his own people.

Dictators

In the event, the Sultan was wrong. Dracula retreated, and his army and nobles deserted him before he could impale them for losing. Terror he inspired, but not loyalty. This was angrily dismissed by Ceaucescu's historians as "treachery". There was nothing wrong with the leader; it was his people who were not up to scratch.

Dracula fled into Hungarian Transylvania, where he expected to be received as a Christian hero, but found himself promptly locked up by the Hungarians for the next ten years. He was a diplomatic embarrassment; Europe could only take him in small doses. He was an unlovable figure, described in a contemporary account as: "Short and stocky, with a cold and terrible appearance. A strong and aquiline nose, swollen nostrils, a thin and reddish face in which very long eyelashes framed large wide open green eyes; the bushy black eyebrows made them appear threatening. His face and chin were shaven, but for a moustache. Swollen temples . . . a bull's neck . . . and black curly locks."

But in 1476, when Wallachia had, in their view, become too pro-Turkish, the Hungarians unleashed their pet Devil-dog once more, and on 26 November, Vlad Dracul III, The Impaler, bounded back onto the throne. The Turks only retreated momentarily and on 26 December, Dracula was killed in battle outside Bucharest. His army of 4,000 was also wiped out. It is strongly rumoured that he was killed by his own officers, or even relatives. His old enemy Mohammed II had the great pleasure of receiving his head, which he displayed proudly on a pole. It was third time lucky for the Sultan. Perhaps this is the origin of the belief that you have to cut off a vampire's head to be properly rid of it.

The rest of Dracula's body was buried outside a church door so that everybody should have the chance to walk on him. Not so, say the Rumanian historians. He was much mourned; it was in fact because he'd married a Roman Catholic and therefore couldn't be buried inside an Orthodox church. A likely story. They claimed to have found his grave at Snagov, Ceaucescu's favourite watering hole. It was by an ironic coincidence that

Vlad Dracul: The Impaler Strikes Back

Nicolae Ceaucescu, who had tried so hard to enhance Dracula's reputation, should have met his death at the same time of the year as his hero, at Christmas, and also at the hands of his own officers; the kind of happy coincidence historians can't prevent.

There was clearly a political and military purpose behind some of Dracula's extraordinary behaviour, but it was not ultimately a success. As he devoted his life to cruelty, we must presume that is how he wished to be remembered; to separate the man from his deeds is opening the way for those who argue that Hitler had nothing to do with the Final Solution.

A typical Rumanian verdict on him in Ceaucescu's time was ". . . a harsh if just man; a brave defender of the independence of his homeland", or "a great hero of the common man. A fighter against wealthy corruption and foreign imperialism . . ." These descriptions are virtually interchangeable with the endless praise the official press heaped upon the head of Ceaucescu. Whatever justification is made for the actions of either of them, their philosophy was one of terror, an obstinately sterile soil in which to cultivate fond memories of oneself.

Chapter Ten

Stalin:
The Bureaucratic Killer

The most ruthless dictator the world has ever seen was not a warlord, like Genghis Khan or Napoleon Bonaparte. In fact, as far as we know – and unlike homicidal maniacs like Idi Amin or the Emperor Caligula – he never personally killed anyone. Joseph Stalin was, first and foremost, a bureaucrat – a paper-shuffler with a heart of cold steel.

After Stalin's death a satirical spoof was published, purportedly a note found among the papers of his head of the secret police, Lavrenty Beria. It read:

> My dear Beria,
> I find that this morning I accidentally mixed up today's list of counter-revolutionary traitors with my list of people to whom I wish to send birthday cards this month, one of the latter being my beloved mother. If you have not already sent the death list out to the execution squads, I would appreciate it if you would remove the birthday list and return it to my office. If, on the other hand, the execution orders have already been carried out, I commend you on your efficiency and suggest you to add your own name to tomorrow's execution list.
>
> Stalin.

A black joke, certainly, but one that neatly depicts the chilling inhumanity of a man who, during the twenty-five years of his rule, ordered or indirectly caused the deaths of tens of millions of his own people.

His original name was Ioseb Dzhugashvilli, and he was born, in 1879, in Georgia: the Caucasus region on the eastern end of the Black Sea and one of the poorest possessions of the Tsarist Russian Empire.

It is likely that some of Ioseb's most striking defining characteristics sprang directly from his upbringing. His dirt-poor, alcoholic father often beat him savagely, teaching the boy the essentials of the "might-makes-right" philosophy that his leadership would later come to epitomize. On the other hand, Ioseb's mother doted on him and insisted that he would one day become a priest (about as high up the Georgian social ladder as the son of a cobbler, like Ioseb, was permitted to climb). His mother's idolizing of him may have instilled Ioseb with the ruthless egotism that was to become the driving force of his nature. And finally, of course, there was Georgia itself: a national culture still deeply infused by the barbaric "law of the blood feud" that taught Ioseb that vengeance, even if delayed by decades, was the finest of sweetmeats.

The boy was sent to a church school and then the Tiflis Theological Seminary, but Ioseb was clearly not – to anyone but his mother's eyes – a natural priest. His brooding, resentful attitude – and his reading of the Communist literature of Karl Marx – got him thrown out when he was eighteen. He then briefly worked as a clerk in the Tiflis Observatory (as far as we know, Dzhugashvilli – the future leader of a worker state and the creator of vast slave labour camps – never did a day of manual labour in his life). But his real calling was revolutionary politics, to which he brought his own brand of brutish but Machiavellian cleverness.

The Caucasus, like most of Tsarist Russia, was in a political ferment around the turn of the nineteenth century. Successive Tsars had ruthlessly tried to stop the empire modernizing and liberalizing, but a growing class of educated peasants, like Dzhugashvilli, could see that the vast majority of the Russian people were being held back in what amounted to medieval serfdom. Most political activism was ruthlessly suppressed by the Tsarist secret police, so Ioseb's decision to go into reformist politics, by joining the Marxist-inspired Social Democrat Party, automatically made him a revolutionary and an outlaw.

Dzhugashvilli was given the job of travelling around the industrial centres of the Caucasus, secretly inciting strikes and civil rights demonstrations by the workers. Unfortunately he soon horrified his superiors by deliberately orchestrating overheated confrontations with the authorities which, all too often, ended in bloodshed. Since Dzhugashvilli made a point of never being caught up in such fights himself, and it was almost always the workers that came off worst from these encounters, word started to go about that he was a police spy and *agent provocateur* – an unproven accusation that would dog him for years.

In 1903, minor reforms offered by the autocratic but vacillating Tsar Nicholas II caused the Social Democrats to split down the middle. On the one side were the liberal Mensheviks, who argued that Russia should aim for a bloodless evolution into a parliamentary democracy and a constitutionally controlled monarchy (much like Britain). On the other side were the radical Bolsheviks, who insisted that – as Karl Marx had predicted – only bloody revolution and the smashing of the exploitative state apparatus could bring true reform. Dzhugashvilli, always inclined to the hands-on approach to politics (provided it was other people who did the actual fighting) naturally plumped for the Bolshevik cause.

The Soviet hagiographers of the Stalin period made much of the following years – claiming that Dzhugashvilli had been one of the foremost Bolshevik revolutionaries in the pre-Great War period. In fact he made slow progress in the Party over the next decade. The double-agent slur seems to have hung over him, holding him back from inner-circle knowledge and position. It didn't help him that, although arrested seven times for revolutionary activity between 1903 and 1913, Dzhugashvilli never received the sort of harsh sentences handed out to others with shorter criminal records. Even the fact that he escaped from prison several times did not improve his reputation – fellow

Bolsheviks whispered that the police had quietly released him in return for his continuing to be a spy for the Tsar.

Dzhugashvilli's big political break came in 1912 when Vladimir Lenin, the exiled leader of the Bolsheviks, promoted him to the Central Committee – the heart of the movement. The reason why Lenin did this is now lost in the myths created by Stalin's later regime, but it seems likely that a leadership void, created by the arrest of a number of high-level Bolsheviks, together with Dzhugashvilli's undeniable skill as an organizer, finally out-balanced his bad reputation.

In celebration, Ioseb Dzhugashvilli changed his name to Joseph Stalin (the surname being a word derived from the Russian word *stal*, meaning "steel"). Like Napoleon before him, Stalin had discovered that a provincial name was a political hindrance, even in a progressive, supposedly egalitarian movement. But he never sought to hide his Caucasian origins; to the end of his life he maintained, and even emphasized, his guttural Georgian accent.

Stalin did not have long to enjoy his new position at the heart of the Party. After a brief period as editor of a new Bolshevik newspaper called *Pravda*, he was arrested again and, in 1913, was sent to life exile in Siberia. He remained there, very much out of the political action, until, in 1917, the very authorities that had banished him themselves fell apart.

In 1906, Nicholas II had reluctantly agreed to allow the formation of a Duma (a limited democratic parliament). This sort of concession might well have saved his throne, if he had not immediately started to undermine the democratic authorities he had just created. When the first and second Dumas, both elected in 1907, returned liberalizing majorities, Nicholas angrily dissolved them – there could be elections, just as long as the Tsar was the only one who could win. This spoilt brat behaviour had the effect of convincing all the reformer factions that he was simply too untrustworthy – that he would always try to take back any reform he might allow.

Then, in 1914, the Russian Empire entered the Great War on

the side of the French and British against the Germans and Austro-Hungarians. Here Nicholas again had a chance to save his throne; as we've seen again and again in this volume, there's nothing like a national emergency to consolidate power for a doubtful or dictatorial government. If Nicholas had managed the war intelligently, he could have won the nation's support but, as usual, he dithered and mismanaged the situation. The results of his incompetence were appalling losses on the battle-front and terrible food shortages at home.

In March 1917, food riots broke out across Petrograd (known today by its original name of St Petersburg). When the capital's garrison, ordered to fire on the starving protestors, refused and instead joined the rioters, Nicholas saw the writing on the wall. He abdicated on 15 March. Just over a year later he, and his entire family, were killed – secretly executed by the Bolsheviks, who feared the imprisoned royal family was about to be rescued by a Tsarist counter-revolutionary army.

Stalin hurried back to Petrograd from Siberia on 25 March 1917, meeting with Lenin, who had also returned from exile. The Bolsheviks were not yet a real power in the hastily formed provisional Government, but over the next months, as the more liberal parties mismanaged matters almost as badly as the Tsar had done, the Bolsheviks built up their support among the urban workers of Petrograd.

On 24 October 1917, the Bolsheviks, backed by the workers, brought about a near-bloodless *coup d'état* (in fact, more people died in accidents during the making of the Soviet movie that celebrated the October Revolution – Eisenstein's *Oktyabr* – than actually died in the revolution itself). The new Marxist Government then immediately made peace with the Germans and set about rebuilding the shattered Russian economy.

Joseph Stalin's organizing role in the revolution had been central, but he soon found himself outshone by Lenin's right-hand man, the intelligent and dashing Leon Trotsky. Stalin, deeply jealous, nevertheless kept his feelings to himself and waited for his opportunity to bring down his opponent.

Stalin: The Bureaucratic Killer

The opportunity did not come for some years. Trotsky, as head of the armed forces, won great Party support for his brilliant handling of the Bolshevik (Red) army in the civil war against the anti-Bolshevik (White) armies in the rest of Russia. Trotsky was also – like Lenin and unlike Stalin – a middle-class intellectual. He could thus build a much closer relationship with the leader than the dull and churlish Stalin ever managed to forge. (In fact, Lenin became quite cold to Stalin after the Georgian made the mistake of insulting Lenin's wife.) But those Party leaders who thought Stalin was just a thickheaded but useful work-donkey, badly misjudged his mental capacity and his quiet determination – and most eventually paid for that misjudgement with their lives.

Using his mastery of bureaucratic matters, Stalin inexorably made himself integral to the structure of the ruling Party (which now called itself *Soviet* rather than Bolshevik). During the two years of civil war (1918–1920) while others, like Trotsky, were winning plaudits for driving out the Whites and defeating several foreign invasions, Stalin gradually took over the mundane, boring, but essential elements of state control. By 1922 he had pulled enough strings and done enough favours to have himself made Secretary General to the Soviet Central Committee. This dull-sounding title actually put Stalin at the heart of the entire governmental system, and henceforth virtually nothing could be enacted without his say-so.

It would have been unlikely that Stalin could have won so much power so quickly, if it were not for the fact that Lenin was very ill. A now generally misjudged figure (thanks largely to viewing him through the bloody lens of the Stalin years) Lenin was not a rabid, all-or-nothing Marxist like China's Mao Zedong or Cambodia's Pol Pot. In fact, in many ways, the Soviet socialist state that Lenin envisioned was closer to the liberal socialism of Britain after the Second World War than it was to the freedom-crushing, absolutist Communism that Stalin would soon create.

Shot in the neck during an assassination attempt in 1918, Lenin had been told that removal of the bullet could be fatal, so it was left in his body. But by 1921 the bullet was clearly killing him anyway, so he had it removed. He initially recovered well from the surgery, and the doctors declared the operation a complete success. Then he suffered several bouts of temporary paralysis down one side of his body, each time worse than the last. Soon everyone, including Lenin, realized that he didn't have long to live. It is possible that either the bullet or the operation caused him fatal spinal nerve damage, but it is also tempting to speculate that someone, using the post-operative period as cover, poisoned Lenin. And the person with most to gain by Lenin's death was, of course, Comrade Secretary General Joseph Stalin.

Lenin dedicated his last painful months to dictating his "testament": a general statement as to where he believed Soviet Russia should go in the future. In it he attacked both Trotsky's plan to forcibly spread Communism to all the capitalist nations of the world *and* Stalin's vision of a monolithic, inward-looking state Communism. More specifically, Lenin called for Stalin to be removed from the post of Secretary General. Seeing, too late, what a viper the quiet Georgian was, it was only his increasing ill health that stopped Lenin pushing through Stalin's political decapitation.

Lenin died in January 1924, and was immediately pseudo-deified by the Party bosses. His corpse was embalmed and laid out, like the relics of a dead saint, as a permanent spectacle for the Soviet masses – a fate that an iconoclast like Lenin would have particularly hated. His call to oust Stalin was also quietly ignored – Stalin was now too powerful a political beast to risk annoying.

Stalin's chief rival, Trotsky, was badly undermined by Lenin's death – a situation that Stalin helped along by making sure that Trotsky was misinformed as to the date of Lenin's "funeral". It may seem petty, but Trotsky's non-attendance at Lenin's farewell ceremony sent his Party popularity crashing, while Stalin – who made sure he was seen to be the chief mourner – suddenly looked to be the most likely to inherit Lenin's mantle of leadership.

Reacting to the swing of popularity, two other Party bigwigs,

Grigory Zinoviev and Lev Kamenev, hurriedly formed a triumvirate leadership with Stalin, ousting Trotsky from the Central Committee. The triumvirate did not last long, however. Stalin dumped the other two as soon as it seemed politically expedient, and formed a pact with right-wing Party bosses Nikolay Bukharin and Aleksey Rykov. Kamenev and Zinoviev were exiled to the political outlands and, as soon as he was sure he could rule the Party and the country on his own, Stalin axed Rykov and Bukharin too. By 1928, the peasant from Georgia was the sole ruler of the whole of the former Russian Empire.

Although it might have seemed a bloodless, bureaucratic coup, Stalin never forgave a former enemy. He eventually killed all those who had stood in his way to ultimate power . . . he just waited until their deaths could further serve his political purposes.

Firmly in control, Stalin abandoned any pretence at following Lenin's plan for liberal Communism, supported by a quasi-capitalist economy. Absolute centralization of power and the state control of every aspect of his people's lives was Stalin's aim. And to achieve it he brutalized the peoples of the USSR more than Tsar Nicholas II and Ivan the Terrible put together. Lethally paranoid, Stalin spent the rest of his life striking out at real and, more often, imagined threats to his leadership. Under the excuse of modernization – which the USSR did indeed sorely need – Stalin put in place programmes that tore the backbone out of Russian life. Most of the peoples of the USSR were muzhiks (peasant farmers). Most of them were very poor, but they owned their own scraps of land and lived in communities and followed a cultural life that was hundreds, even thousands of years old. Stalin ordered all these small farms and many of the communities to be liquidated. Their former owners were to now work the land on vast "collective" farms, under direct government control. Those that refused – called kulaks by the Party – were executed on the spot or transported to vast slave labour camps (gulags) where they, and often their whole families, were starved and worked to death.

Dictators

A similar fate was handed out, almost arbitrarily, to whole racial groups – especially those, on the outer regions of the Soviet Empire, who were difficult to control centrally. Stalin took it for granted that those not firmly in his grip must be plotting counter-revolutions, and a lack of any supporting evidence simply indicated, to his skewed logic, just how devious the plotters must be. So – taking the view that it was better that a hundred innocent people should suffer, rather than one guilty person should escape – he set out to break the Soviet-Russian peoples *en masse*.

Draconian laws were passed, making it almost impossible for even the most upstanding and cautious citizen to keep a totally clean record sheet. Thus, if the authorities wanted to punish someone, for whatever reason, they could always find an infringement of one sort or another; and as with individuals, so it was with the inhabitants of villages, towns or regions. The enforced transport of entire populations to the underpopulated but murderously harsh Siberian steppes caused the deaths of hundreds of thousands. (Exile to Siberia had been a common punishment under the Tsars, as we've seen in Stalin's own case, but it was never utilized on such a monstrous scale.) And among those especially marked out for harsh treatment were the peoples of the Caucasus. Stalin might have been proud of his Georgian accent, but that didn't stop him brutalizing his own people. His callous cruelty left a legacy of hate and a blood-debt that still poisons the region and its relations with Russia today.

Officially, everything was now owned collectively. What that actually meant was that everything and everyone in Stalin's Russia was owned by the state – by the "eternal Party" and, ultimately, by "Papa Stalin" himself. Karl Marx's vision of a workers' Utopia, free of want and with all standing equal, was translated into an absolutist dictatorship, in which everyone but the leader was effectively a slave under a suspended sentence of death.

The collectivization of Soviet agriculture proved to be an unmitigated disaster. Harvest yields plummeted as the largely uneducated and untrained muzhiks struggled with the new conditions. Many were exiled to Siberian gulags or shot for failing to fulfil the impossible quotas set by party bureaucrats. There was even a widespread famine in the Ukraine – formerly the "breadbasket" of the Russian Empire. Instead of rushing grain stocks to the famine area, however, Stalin let the Ukrainians starve while he continued to export the very foodstuffs that were in such desperately short supply.

It was important for the USSR's image abroad, he said, that the difficulties in Soviet farming (which he put down to kulak sabotage) should not be revealed: thus the exports to foreign nations continued, sent along with faked reports of enormous Soviet food overproduction. At least ten million people died as a direct result of Stalin's agricultural policies during the years it took to get collectivization working (which it never fully did – up to the collapse of Soviet Communism, the USSR was still having to buy in vast amounts of food from the USA and the European Union).

At the same time that most of the USSR was either on short rations or starving, Stalin ordered a "five-year plan" to modernize Soviet industry. This was less disastrous than the collectivization of the farms but, despite the mass education policies started in Lenin's day, most of the Russian population simply were not ready to create an instant industrial revolution. At every point when some largely arbitrary quota was missed, it was taken as read that saboteurs had caused the problem. In some cases, managers and workers were arrested and tortured until they "confessed" to their crimes. Then, after a much publicized "show trial", they were executed. But usually people just needed to be accused of "counter-revolutionary activities" – whatever the evidence – to be immediately taken out and shot.

Again, as with the deaths of millions of kulaks, there are no surviving records as to just how many industrial workers were killed for such imagined acts of sabotage. But the list of the murdered industrial workers almost certainly ran into the hundreds of thousands.

Dictators

All this death should have undoubtedly led to a revolution or a coup and, quite possibly, the dictator's own messy demise. But Stalin was a visionary in at least one sense: he knew just how effective fear, spread with modern communications, could be as a breaker of men's spirits.

Throughout the 1920s and 1930s, Stalin built up the Soviet secret police – variously titled, at different times, the Cheka, the GPU, the OGPU, NKVD and, most infamously, the KGB. The men and women of the secret police soon became a state within a state – a vast and parasitic growth that existed to find (or invent) treasonous activity, and thus justify further extending its own power. To the secret police, the true enemies were not the capitalist powers (who certainly did try to attack and undermine Communism at every opportunity) but the Soviet people themselves. Implicated in Stalin's innumerable murders, the secret police were well aware that only the public's ignorance, patriotism and fear kept them from turning on their oppressors, so they used every opportunity to instil all three.

Simply showing interest in forbidden matters (such as religion or foreign travel) or suggesting the slightest doubt towards the policies of Stalin and the Party was deemed as enough reason for lengthy gulag imprisonment or execution. And to collect such damning information, the secret police ruthlessly encouraged friends to inform on their friends, wives to inform on their husbands and children to inform on their parents. Almost everyone within the Soviet fortress state became implicated, more or less directly, with their own oppression and brutalization – and the only way to escape the guilt of such an association was to deny it was happening at all: a schizophrenic state of self-delusion that George Orwell – in *1984*, his satire on totalitarianism – called "doublethink".

Love of "Mother Russia" was espoused by every newsreel, every movie and by every newspaper (despite the fact that the majority of Soviet citizens were not actually Russian, but were Belorussian, Ukrainian, Moldavian, Turkmen, Siberian or Caucasian). But above this patriotism came the near deification of Comrade Stalin – "the man of steel". Of course, every god needs a devil, so Stalin put his old animosities to work for him.

In 1934, Sergey Kirov – Stalin's former rival and ally, but now very far from any position of power – was shot dead by an unknown assassin in Leningrad (formerly Petrograd, formerly St Petersburg). Nikita Khrushchev, a later General Secretary of the USSR and the first Soviet leader to denounce the "Cult of Stalin", hinted after Stalin's death that Kirov had been murdered on Stalin's orders. True or not, Stalin used the death of Kirov as an excuse to begin the political "purges" that were to send millions more Soviet citizens to their deaths.

Stalin might have regretted simply exiling his old opponent, Leon Trotsky, back in 1929. But after Kirov's murder, Stalin used his former rival's continued existence, living and writing in Mexico, to insist that there was an international plot to destroy himself, "the Great Leader", (and thus the USSR itself), masterminded by the "Arch Traitor", Leon Trotsky.

Two other former allies, Zinoviev and Kamenev, were dragged out of their enforced obscurity, forced to confess to ludicrous treason charges, were put on show trial, then were shot. As other prominent Party officials – all from the old Lenin days – were put through the same ordeal, it soon became clear that Stalin was killing off all those who had been part of the regime before he came to absolute power. All those, in short, that he had ever had a reason to resent. In doing this Stalin was not only indulging his own taste for protracted revenge but, while still claiming to venerate Lenin, destroying any remaining aspect of Lenin's vision for the USSR.

The political purges continued throughout the 1930s. Not only Stalin, but any Party official with a grudge could use the witch hunt as an excuse to settle old scores. Soon people were accusing others simply to pre-empt the possibility of an accusation coming the other way. In this way at least as many loyal Stalinists died as did members of the "old guard". Probably more than eight million people died in the Stalinist purges but, again, there are no accurate figures because the records were deliberately destroyed by subsequent Soviet regimes.

Having run out of personal scores to settle, Stalin turned his attention to any group who might conceivably be a threat to him. And, inevitably, his eyes turned to the vast Red Army – about the only force left in the USSR that could take on his secret police and win. In less than three years – between 1937 and 1939 – almost every officer in the Soviet army, from field marshals down to humble lieutenants, was accused of treason. Most of them were shot or were exiled to slow death in the gulags.

This monstrous and unnecessary decapitation of the Soviet fighting forces goes to prove that Stalin had his eyes too firmly fixed on internal control of the USSR, and not enough on foreign affairs. In Germany, Hitler and the Nazis had come to power and had used many of Stalin's totalitarian tricks – the worship of the nation, the semi-deification of the leader and the ruthless crushing of any internal political threat. By 1939, German armies stood poised to invade the rest of Europe and, inevitably, the USSR. In fact Hitler had been foolish enough to point this out in his political treatise *Mein Kampf*: Russia was to be the bread-basket of the Greater German Reich, worked by those "subhuman" Russian inhabitants that German slave masters allowed to live.

Finally realizing the peril, Stalin surprised the world by striking a pact with Hitler – with the conquered and subdivided Poland as the agreement table. Both sides were, of course, playing for time: Hitler to build up his forces enough to conquer the USSR, and Stalin to train officers for his huge, but leaderless, army. Hitler won the race, and invaded the Soviet Union on 22 June 1941.

Stalin, who had ignored all warnings that the attack was imminent, reacted in his usual manner. The commander of the beleaguered western front and his entire command staff were immediately arrested and shot. The men of the – again – leaderless Red Army were slaughtered in their millions and the Germans got as far as the outskirts of Moscow before winter and

Siberian snow troops threw them back. Stalin, to give him his due, refused to leave the Soviet capital, even when it seemed likely to be captured, giving great hope to the defenders. But he had also allowed himself a little treat: Leon Trotsky had become unnecessary as the chief external bogeyman, now that Hitler had applied for the job, so Stalin finally gave his vengeance full reign and had his old adversary assassinated in 1940.

The defeat of Germany was a long, savage business, costing the lives of 8.6 million Red Army soldiers and the "collateral" deaths of nearly 17 million Soviet civilians. Certainly the blame for this sea of blood can't all be laid at Stalin's door, but his butchering of the Soviet military command structure, and his insistence – like Hitler – of personally, and often ineptly, directing forces at the front via radio, certainly cost the lives of millions of people who might otherwise have survived the war.

One of the victims of Stalin's poor war record was his own son, Jacob. Always despised by his father – as Stalin's father had apparently despised young Ioseb – Jacob had once attempted suicide, after which Stalin wrote him off as a weakling. During the war the Germans captured Jacob and offered to exchange him for captured German prisoners, but Stalin curtly refused the offer. Jacob died in a Nazi prison camp and his wife and children were sent to a Siberian slave labour camp. But in ordering this, Stalin would have argued he was simply being egalitarian. The families of captured Soviet soldiers were routinely thrown into the gulags as a warning to other soldiers at the front – as were those pathetically few Soviet survivors who, after the war, lived to return from Nazi internment.

The ruthless imprisonment of his own daughter-in-law and grandchildren was not atypical of Stalin's treatment of his family. His first wife, Ekaterina – Jacob's mother – died only three years after their marriage in 1903, so did not live to see her husband become a total monster. Stalin's second wife, Nadiezhada, whom he married in 1919, was not so lucky. She made the mistake, in the late 1920s, of pleading with him to be a more humane leader, after which he treated her with such cold derision that she eventually killed herself. His son by Nadiezhada, Vasily, was given an important job in the Soviet air force, but his father made it plain to everyone that he thought him totally worthless. Vasily eventually drank himself to death. The last immediate member of Stalin's family was his daughter by Nadiezhada, Svetlana. To her Stalin would sometimes show smothering affection, but at other times he would terrify her with furious and sometimes violent fits of rage. She survived her father, but remained emotionally scarred for the rest of her life.

The end of the Second World War saw the USA and the USSR raised to the position of the world's last two surviving super-powers. With hindsight, it might seem inevitable that two such dialectically opposed ideologies would eventually become enemies but, at the time, there was genuine hope that peace and harmony was within their grasp: after all, hadn't they just co-operated in defeating fascism?

For several decades Western historians blamed Stalin for the post-war political decay into the Cold War. Certainly it is true that he had no intention of giving up the Eastern European states, like Poland and Hungary, that the Red Army had captured from the Germans at such cost. Yet, documents revealed by the US Freedom of Information Act in the 1970s, show that it was a betrayal by the Western powers that initially and permanently soured relations with the USSR.

President Roosevelt and Prime Minister Churchill had promised Stalin at the Yalta Conference in 1945 that the defeated Germany would be held permanently under Allied military control, so that the threat of a "Fourth Reich" could never overshadow Europe and the USSR. However, Roosevelt died shortly thereafter and his replacement, Truman (with Churchill's agreement) reneged on the agreement and started to politically rebuild West Germany – the area under US, French and British control – openly aiming towards full German independence as soon as possible.

Stalin saw this as a straight case of betrayal and never trusted the West again. As a result he instigated bullying policies, such as the Berlin Blockade, that allowed Western politicians to paint him as a warmonger. In fact, war was the furthest thing from Stalin's mind: the USSR was sapped by the war on Germany, and had enough to do holding down the territories it had just conquered. But, through Stalin's habitual pigheaded brutality, President Truman and the White House economists got what they wanted – a permanent, but essentially harmless monster (this was before the USSR got the atom bomb) to frighten the voters with. This allowed, in 1947, the setting up of a "Security State" through the Congressional "National Security Act": a perpetual if unofficial state of emergency in the US. This, in turn, allowed the continuance of the high-output "war economy" that had turned America into a superpower in the first place. The Cold War was started just as deliberately as Hitler's attack on the USSR had been and, arguably, with the same purpose: to create a world empire founded on endless conflict. (See Gore Vidal's historical essay, "The Last Empire" (*Vanity Fair*, November 1997).)

Stalin's final years were less savage than his earlier rule. But the purges continued, although at a reduced scale, and the peoples of the USSR remained slaves of the State in all but name. The new aim of the Stalinist regime was to deride all things foreign – and especially Western – as decadent and subversive. More than ever, Stalin's Russia became an inward-looking, self-deluding fortress state.

Perhaps the greatest irony of Stalin's monstrous life was its end. In January 1953, Stalin ordered the arrest of a number of leading Soviet doctors. The seventy-four-year-old dictator was, after a period of comparative tranquillity, showing all the signs of increased paranoia that would inevitably lead to a new set of purges. The doctors had been arrested on charges of poisoning a number of leading Party members – the implication being that those in power had ordered their deaths in order to take their places. Stalin was clearly planning to start the new round of executions by killing the top Party bosses.

Stalin died suddenly on 5 March 1953. It is probable –

although it has never been proved – that the Kremlin doctors, egged on by terrified Party bosses, poisoned him. The fear he instilled in all levels of Soviet society might have been his own death warrant.

Thanks to the destruction of records by the Soviet authorities, it is also now impossible to know how many of his own people Stalin caused to die by torture, execution, starvation, exposure and exhaustion. A conservative estimate is around 30 to 40 million.

Chapter Eleven

Saddam Hussein: The Butcher of Baghdad

The 28 April 1992 was President Saddam Hussein's fifty-fifth birthday. It is over a year since the "Mother of all Battles" and the spectacular rout of the Iraqi forces in Kuwait. Contrary to hopes, Saddam Hussein is firmly back in power. In his home town of Takrit, north of Baghdad, columns of carefully organized demonstrators chant "We all love Saddam", and "Our blood, our soul, we sacrifice to Saddam!". The eighty-mile road from Baghdad is clogged with lorries bussing in more demonstrators, under the supervision of officials of the ruling Baath party. They are herded into the football stadium to watch colourfully dressed folk dancers perform a piece entitled "The village hears of the birth of Saddam". Various government dignitaries watch, mostly relatives of Saddam Hussein. There is only one significant absence; the birthday boy himself. He is notoriously elusive, and like a God, can only be worshipped via his many priests and images. It is not divine inscrutability that makes him so aloof, but fear of assassination. As compensation for his physical absence the impression is given that he is everywhere and everybody. His portrait, dressed as sober statesman, military genius, historic conqueror or even telephone engineer is plastered all over Baghdad. His name is mentioned on the radio every minute of the day. He is constantly on television, but cannot give live interviews or an off-the-cuff response to events as his speeches are filmed hours or days beforehand in secret locations, for fear of betraying his whereabouts to the agents and aircraft of his enemies. The Israelis have sworn to be revenged for the random rocket attacks on their country during the war.

Dictators

Saddam Hussein. *Popperfoto*

Inside Iraq, the Kurdish and Shia populations hate him; the enthusiasm that surrounds his personality cult is orchestrated. Iraq is a police state.

By still clinging to power after a decade of disastrous warfare, worsening social conditions, internal repression and the systematic murder of minorities, Saddam Hussein qualified himself as one of the world's great dictators. As slippery and tough as a cockroach, and entirely without shame, he exhibited the callous lack of emotion and preference for solving problems with violence that one would expect of an ambitious mobster. Which is how he started out, and where he cultivated his instinct to survive at any cost; hell would be playing Monopoly with Saddam Hussein. So erratic and unrealistic is his behaviour, that in an effort to understand what zany clock makes him tick, one Western security service came up with the theory that the drugs he takes for angina have the side effect of making him feel invulnerable.

He was born in 1937, in Al Ouja, a village outside Takrit. He remains proud of his humble origin in a mud hut, in the midst of a poor, water-melon-growing Sunni community. Iraq is an overwhelmingly Moslem society, but within it there are innumerable religious and tribal groups. Sunni Moslems, the majority orthodox doctrine of Islam generally, form only a fifth of Iraq's population. Saddam himself, nominally Sunni, used religion only as a political tool, posing hypocritically as an Islamic hero in his efforts to present his opposition to the West as a Holy War. His weakness for cigars, scotch and adultery was too well known for the sight of him kneeling in prayer to be taken seriously.

His father died before he was born. The gossip was that he was illegitimate. As Saddam developed his later obsession with history, he claimed that he was the illegitimate child of the Iraqi Hashemite King, through which he traced his direct descent from the Prophet Mohammed himself.

His mother re-married, and Saddam was raised in the house of his stepfather, Ibrahim al Hassan, who delighted in beating the boy remorselessly. With the shadow of his rumoured illegitimacy hanging over him, Saddam was an outcast in the impoverished but custom-bound society. As he walked to school in Takrit, he carried a steel bar to protect himself from the other boys. His only allies were his cousin, Adnan Khairallah, rewarded for his kindness by a future position as Defence Minister, and his uncle, Khairallah Tulfah, who became

Governor of Baghdad. Tulfah was a monstrous bigot, who wrote a tract proposing that there are "three who God should not have created; Persians, Jews and flies". Adnan eventually went the way of all flesh, when, after complaining about Saddam's blatant infidelity to his wife, who was Adnan's sister, he died in a helicopter crash.

They were small-time gangsters, feared as local brigands. In his search for acceptance and prestige, Saddam was inevitably drawn into their web of corruption, crime and murder. At the age of ten, Saddam's cousins gave him his first real possession; a revolver. In his young teens, he committed his first killings on Tulfah's behalf. By the time he moved to Baghdad in the late 1950s, he had a considerable reputation as a thug and assassin.

He enrolled in law school, but crime kept him too busy to attend. In 1957, at the age of twenty-one, he joined the Baath Party, a tiny fledgling movement espousing the creation of a single Arab state. Anti-Western, anti-Persian and anti-Jewish, it was a synthesis of Arab nationalism and socialism founded by a Syrian secondary school teacher, Michel Alfaq. Saddam became highly useful as a hit-man and tough enforcer in the Baath Party's violent opposition to the Hashemite monarchy. Having backed the military overthrow of the King, the Baath then sought to subvert the new government by assassinating the President, Brigadier Qassem.

Saddam Hussein was one of an eight-man hit squad selected for the task. They planned to shoot up Qassem's car as he drove between his house and his office at the Defence Ministry. When the plan finally went into operation on 7 October 1959, it was a total farce. One of the assassins was supposed to use his car to block the street and force Qassem's car to a halt, Unfortunately, he lost his keys, and while the would-be killers fell to arguing about whose fault it was, Qassem arrived at the destined spot. They managed to shoot the driver, but in the cross-fire, the successful marksman was then shot dead by his comrades. Several others, including Saddam, also wounded each other. The assassins hobbled off, convinced that some of the mass of flying lead must have hit Qassem. The debacle was re-written when Saddam came to power as a mass-battle against overwhelming odds, in which Saddam, although grievously wounded, was the hero, pulling cannon-shell out of his leg with a pair of scissors. The doctor who actually treated him remembers a tiny super-ficial wound. Needless to say, the doctor later fled Iraq when he discovered a huge bomb under his car.

Whilst his fellow assassins were rounded up, Saddam escaped to Syria and then moved to Egypt where he spent the next few years, manoeuvring his way into the inner circles of the exiled Baath movement. The Egyptians were generally sympathetic towards the Baath, but distrusted the naked ambition of Saddam.

In 1963, the Baath took power in Iraq in a bloody coup, and Saddam returned as a gun-toting bodyguard on the right of the Party. He won favour and fear by his willingness to dispose of opponents by the most direct methods. He even offered to blow away the leader of the Party's left faction, then Deputy Premier. His offer was politely refused by Hassan-al-Bakr, his boss, who didn't want to set a precedent he guessed he might fall victim to.

The Baath were turfed out of power by the army, disgusted at the violence and chaotic in-fighting. Going underground suited Saddam Hussein. This was the kind of electioneering he under-stood, proceeding via violence and intrigue. Saddam was never without a machine-gun and at least one revolver. In this environment he flourished. Michel Alfaq thought his limited skills particularly appropriate to the Baath's need for violence rather than diplomacy, and supported his claim to the position of Secretary and Leader. The job was to be shared. His co-appointee, Abdel al Shaikhili, was later purged and murdered. It was an unprecedented appointment, as he had no credentials and no experience, and was not accepted by the rest of the Party. Saddam would have to resort to his customary methods to achieve power.

In 1966, Saddam seized the post of Deputy Secretary General

at gunpoint, and began to build up a net-work of intimates dependent upon him for favour. These were usually his relatives, or failing that, from his home town of Takrit. He was known to the public only as a lowly gunman, entirely uncultured, vulgar and with a complete absence of moral values. Yet, he had a growing fascination for history, particularly the great figures of the mythic Arab past, and began to see himself as a man of destiny, following in the footsteps of Nebuchadnezzar, the enslaver of Israel and Emperor of Babylon.

In 1968, the Baath returned to power in another coup. Saddam's forthright abilities earned him the position of Deputy President. Hassan-al-Bakr, the President, needed his sheer ruthlessness to create a Baathist State. He was the power behind the throne, instrumental in implementing the policies of repression and terror that evolved. He established a "Department of Internal Security", the official state torture-service, run by Nadlum Kazar, a notorious psychopath who ran the central interrogation unit at Qasr al Nihayyah in Baghdad. It was there, in 1973, that a survivor saw Saddam Hussein, Deputy President of Iraq, bodily pick up a still struggling prisoner and toss him into a vat of acid, watching fascinated as the wriggling man dissolved.

The Baath State that Saddam inevitably inherited on 16 July 1979 was well on the way to being run on the only emotional lines he understood, those of terror. He had systematically eradicated everyone who posed a threat, real or imagined, to him, often with his own hands. He was quite happy to take part in torture. Yet unlike his over-enthusiastic sons, who regarded rape and torture as family perks, there seems little evidence that Saddam sadistically enjoyed killing people; for him it was simply part of maintaining his power – all in a day's work. During the war with Iran, with Iraq in pieces, Saddam, feeling insecure, suggested to his ministers that he might step down. Most took the hint, disagreed and began to flatter him as required. His health minister, Riaz Hussein, foolishly took him at his word and said he would be happy to accept Saddam's resignation. Saddam promptly dragged him into the next room, shot him, and had his dismembered body returned to his wife in a carrier bag. As one former official said of Hussein: "You quickly realize that he trusts absolutely no one. Everyone is a potential enemy. Sometimes you see him with children, and he is smiling and stroking their hair. That's because they are no threat to him."

Under Saddam, torture became a customary experience, used not to extract information, but to re-model the very thoughts of the populace. Thus, torturers saw themselves as creative artists, engineers of the human soul. Exacting confessions to non-existent crimes is a means of compelling victims to surrender their individuality, to accept without question the truth as presented by the State. In order to heighten the impression of an organization as omniscient and divine as its leader and to cultivate the necessary sense of sin and guilt within the people, the security services were anonymous and selected victims at random. No explanations were offered; the event was efficiently calculated to suggest unimaginable horrors. As Samir al Khalil, Iraqi dissident and author wrote: "The pattern is for agents to pick someone up from work, or at night from his house . . . what one assumes to be the corpse is brought back weeks or maybe months later and delivered to the head of the family in a sealed box. A death certificate is produced for signature to the effect that the person has died of fire, swimming or other such accidents. Someone is allowed to accompany the police and box for a ceremony, but at no time are they allowed to see the corpse. The cost of proceedings is demanded in advance . . ."

Acid baths were commonly used to make thousands of corpses disappear. Amnesty International detailed thirty methods of torture used in Iraq, from beating to mutilation, from rape to electrocution, including the gouging out of eyes, the cutting off of noses, breasts, penises and limbs. Heavy-metal poisoning was a favoured means of killing off undesirables. Lead and thallium were administered to prisoners in soft drinks during uneventful but deliberately prolonged interrogation. Children were routinely tortured to extract confessions from their parents. In 1985, three hundred children were held at Fusailiyya Prison, where they were whipped, sexually abused and given electric shocks. In order to assist their work, the security forces became master players of the rumour machine. They used it to create the enemy within, which they must flush out, and then used it again to spread rumours of the horrendous punishments that traitors faced. A constant stream of videos showing confessions, trials and executions were released to the public. Baath officials were required to take part in executions and were filmed doing so, thus binding themselves together in responsibility with "blood cement".

It was with the application of this mafia-style ideology of shared guilt that Saddam Hussein opened his account as President. A couple of nights after taking office, he hosted a dinner party for senior Baath officials. After the meal, he casually suggested that they all jot down details of any meetings they might have had with two of their colleagues, Muhie Abdel Hussein and Mohamed Ayesb. He gave no explanation. The following day he informed the Baath Revolutionary Council that the two named officials were the ringleaders of a plot to overthrow the regime. Fortunately, he added, he was in possession of a complete list of their fellow conspirators. With crocodile tears streaming down his face, he read out a list compiled from among his dinner party guests. It included several of the highest ranking officials and a quarter of the Revolutionary Council. The Baath leadership was subsequently invited to accompany Saddam to where their former colleagues were now held. There, they were issued with guns, and along with Saddam formed the firing squad. The Secret Police stood behind them, to provide an added spur to their loyalty.

Iraq is potentially a prosperous country. It has vast oil reserves and healthy agricultural resources. Like many of the Middle Eastern nations its size, borders and very existence are a consequence of colonial influence and World War. The Baath Movement, which never exerted much influence outside Iraq and for a brief time Syria, had its roots in the desire for the collective Arab nation, so long kicked about by the colonial superpowers, to assert themselves as a force on the world stage. Since President Nasser of Egypt, the Arabs have looked for a strong representative and spokesman for all, not just the small, incredibly rich and pro-Western oil states, whose wealth is often bitterly resented among the poorer nations. It is this vacancy that Saddam Hussein had his eye on.

In 1979, the Shah of Iran was overthrown and Iran became a strictly Muslim and violently anti-Western country. The conflict between the Arabs and Persians is historic, and there has been a long-standing dispute over territory between Iran and Iraq. Saddam thought he would be able to take advantage of the instability in Iran to launch a swift smash and grab as a prelude to Imperial expansion. Saddam was confident the war would be over in a fortnight. He was certain Iraq had the hardware. It had been shopping worldwide for the best the arms trade could offer. Throughout the following conflict, the West began to favour and actively support Iraq with arms and finance. America, finding itself in bitter opposition to the Iranian regime, thought Saddam an attractive prospect. It has recently been revealed that George Bush Senior's administration were still supplying economic aid, intelligence and advanced weapons technology to "The Butcher of Baghdad" two months before he invaded Kuwait.

Iran had a seemingly endless supply of eager Muslim heroes. Ayatollah Khomeini promised anyone who died for Iran would be perishing as a Muslim martyr. Large numbers of young Iranians seemed to be happy to commit suicide in the cause, jogging up to the frontline carrying their own coffins. The Ayatollah called for an army of twenty million. The Iranians seemed indifferent to the loss of life. In two attacks in the Basra region alone they lost 100,000 men and boys. The war became a hideous, life-consuming stalemate, and a jamboree for the arms trade.

By the third week of the war, Saddam was turning on Iranian

civilian targets. Military spending rocketed. The hardware was inefficiently used, with Iraqi gunners frequently shooting down their own aircraft. In the first six years of this awful, pointless conflict, France alone sold $15–17 billion of military hardware to the Iraqis. Saddam had to find ways of killing more Iranians faster. By 1984 Iraq was using mustard and nerve gas against the Iranians. Reporters could not believe the scale of the carnage. On the battlefield, soldiers no older than children tore at each other with their bare hands. The rivers and swamps were clogged with bodies.

When he became leader of Iraq, Saddam had no military experience whatsoever. His gangland, bar-room, bottle-in-the-face tactics in both his disastrous wars displayed his failure to grasp any military tactics. He compensated by portraying himself to the public as a great military leader to demonstrate he was in charge. Huge portraits showed him in permanent uniform, armed to the teeth. His whole cabinet dressed as soldiers. This backfired when it became apparent that the war was a complete cock-up.

As a gangster, Saddam had fought personal battles with his opponents, using whatever means came to hand to survive, be it broken bottle or gun. He has no notion of the "last resort". He used gas, not because it was a last ditch effort, but because it was an effective weapon to kill his enemies. If he had possessed nuclear weapons, either then or during the subsequent war in Kuwait, he would have used them without compunction. During the war with Iran, Iraq developed military applications for typhoid, cholera, anthrax, and equine encephalitis. Much of the research was underwritten by Western banks. Gas was used on his own deserters. In spite of this chamber of horrors, the war dragged on until September 1988.

When it finished, with nearly two million dead, Iraq was at least $80 billion in the red. Furthermore, it ended without victory and with the Iranians in the ascendant. This didn't stop Saddam declaring himself the victor, and raising monuments and awarding himself an endless string of titles to prove it.

Saddam Hussein: The Butcher of Baghdad

Towards the end of the war he had rounded on the Kurdish minority in the north of Iraq. At Halabja, in March 1988, 5,000 civilians were killed, in what was the first documented use of nerve gas in history. His intention was to depopulate Kurdistan, a traditional bastion of resistance, whilst attention was still on the fighting at the front. By mid-1989, he had destroyed 4,000 Kurdish settlements. A British documentary film-maker managed to smuggle out conclusive evidence of the atrocities; bodies lay piled high in desolate villages, a film over their eyes and a horrible slime pouring out of their noses and mouths, their skin peeling and bubbling. An American Senator tried to introduce the "Prevention of Genocide Act", but Reagan's Government squashed it, still thinking its interests lay in keeping Saddam sweet.

Having, as he saw it, beaten Iran, all Saddam needed now was to turf Israel out of Palestine to make himself the great Arabian hero that, in believing his own publicity, he imagined himself destined to be. Here was an irony; whilst killing the Kurds, he compared himself to the greatest of Kurdish heroes and scourge of the Crusaders, Saladin. He began to rebuild Babylon, having each brick stamped with his mark, as Nebuchadnezzar had done. Around the country, there were over eighty palaces for his personal use. The rumour spread that he was in fact the illegitimate offspring of the Hashemite King Ghazi. It was thought he might declare himself a monarch, an incongruous decision for a once revolutionary, socialist, rabid anti-monarchist to take. It was all part of making the people somehow think that if he was a hero, they must have won.

In reality, having fought a losing, costly draw, social unrest began to spread, and with a tide of several million idle soldiers slopping around the country, Saddam needed another national cause fast to preserve his position. He needed a real victory.

In order to further his plans against Israel, which he openly threatened to burn to destruction, he required money to buy conventional weapons and develop nuclear and biological ones. The need became greater after the Israelis, who have learned to

Dictators

take seriously what other countries dismiss as mere rhetoric, bombed his nuclear facilities. Saddam's theory for removing Israel was indicative of how little he valued human life. Israel's precious resource is its people. It could not afford to fight a long, corpse-laden war, such as Saddam is fond of. With such a war draining Israel of human life, immigration would dry up and the nation vanish. It didn't matter how many Iraqis it took.

He needed money, but with these huge debts, his country would be paying off its loans for years. To cap Saddam's problems, but also to provide him with the excuse he needed, the price of oil slumped and with it Iraq's income. He rounded on the Gulf oil-producing states, in particular, Kuwait, which had given and lent him millions of dollars to fight Iran. He accused the small states of keeping the oil price low by over-producing, and hence "harming even the milk our children drink". He demanded that Iraq's debts be written off. As Saddam saw it, he had seen off the Persian threat on their behalf. In Kuwait's case, he unearthed an old territorial dispute over two islands in the Gulf.

The scene was set for the Mother of all Battles. In August 1990, Saddam invaded Kuwait. To the moment the first bombs started falling on Baghdad, he never believed that the Allies would go to war. He told the US Ambassador: "Yours is a society which cannot accept 10,000 dead in one battle."

The West, forever in a terrible tangle over its relations in the Middle East and what to make of Saddam, breathed a sigh of relief. At last they knew what he was: a good, old-fashioned imperialist dictator with genocidal tendencies.

Saddam had been obliged to fall in love with himself so much, he firmly believed that the Arab coalition which formed against him would fall apart, that its people would rise to acclaim him as the leader of the Arab world and overthrow their governments. Hence he turned to firing missiles at Israeli cities, to turn what was, for both sides, a war about politics and oil into one about race. It failed. Israel stayed out and the Allies stayed cemented together by cash and a common purpose. Saddam's behaviour, using hostages and prisoners for human shields and propaganda purposes, was a big mistake. Far from frightening people, it gave impetus to what was an initially shaky cause. It was, yet again, the misapplication of small-time mob tactics in the big arena. It looked awful.

Saddam's army of a million men was humiliated in a ground war lasting a mere four days. His hardware was destroyed. Little surprise then, that Saddam's regime came close to falling in the months after the war. Egged on by promises of American military support, the Marsh Arabs in the south of Iraq and the Kurds in the north staged simultaneous revolts. The Americans then had second thoughts; they had belatedly realized that if they helped totally defeat Saddam, they would be positioning themselves to the open-ended burden of having to run Iraq. In 1998, ex-President George Bush Senior wrote, in his book *A World Transformed*, that: "Trying to eliminate Saddam would have incurred incalculable human and political costs . . . We would have been forced to occupy Baghdad and, in effect, rule Iraq. There was no viable exit strategy we could see . . . Had we gone the invasion route, [we] could conceivably still be an occupying power in a bitterly hostile land."

So Bush Senior's Government reneged on their promise to back the anti-Saddam rebellions and – often literally watched by US troops just across the borders – Saddam's security forces put down the uprisings with mass arrests, executions and strafing runs on undefended villages with attack helicopters and fighter jets. Uncounted thousands died or were driven from their homes before, very belatedly, the Western powers set up "no-fly zones": areas protected by Western air forces that Saddam's military had to move through with great caution and circumspection.

The United Nations imposed economic sanctions on the still defiant Hussein regime. The Iraqis were blocked from selling crude oil – their only exportable commodity – in the hope that Saddam would become too broke to rearm his shattered army. The result, predictably, was that he took money from wherever he could to rearm, leaving his people desperately hungry and devoid of proper amenities and even basic medicines. Iraq, having once boasted an excellent medical service, soon had the world's highest percentage of infant mortalities. Not that this bothered the UN and the US too much. Representatives openly admitted that they hoped the unnecessary misery in Iraq would lead to "regime change': a successful revolution.

It did not. For over a decade Saddam Hussein remained defiant, sometimes deliberately breaching UN sanctions. Occasional US cruise missile attacks on Baghdad, as retaliation, did not cause the people to rise up against the Baathists and, some noticed, these cruel but militarily useless attacks seemed to always take place when either President Bush Senior or his successor, Bill Clinton, were getting low opinion polls at home . . . the explosions in Baghdad suburbs *did* make excellent viewing on the television news.

Yet it would be wrong to say that everyone in George Bush Senior's administration was against ousting Sadam in 1990. When George Bush Junior took possession of the White House in 2001, he reinstalled several of these old warhorses. The US invasion of Iraq (backed by an embarrassingly small "coalition of the willing") took place on 20 March 2003.

The reasons given for the invasion of Iraq – suspected weapons of mass destruction concealed by Saddam and/or Iraqi involvement in the September 11, 2001 attacks on New York and Washington DC by the Islamic terrorist group, Al Queda – have since been proved to be incorrect: the result of "misjudged intelligence reports". Embarrassed politicians then switched to claiming that "regime change" had also been a motivating factor, but given that, often, the same people had enthusiastically backed Saddam Hussein through the worst years of his dictatorship, the public took this explanation with a pinch of salt. Drilling rights to Iraq's vast crude oil reserves – just as it became evident that the world was starting to run out of oil – was what many thought the invasion had really been about.

The attack went better than anyone could have hoped, with

Saddam's broken conscript army surrendering more often than they fought, but the aftermath was terrible. Even though Saddam Hussein was eventually captured (literally hiding in a hole) the seemingly endless killing of Iraqi civilians, caught in the crossfire between occupation troops and Islamic militants, horrified the world.

The playwright Bertolt Brecht once commented (about the defeat of Hitler):

Don't rejoice in his death, you men.
For, although the world stood up and stopped the bastard,
The bitch that bore him is in heat again.

The Butcher of Baghdad may be gone, but the agonies of Iraq spawned countless new butchers.